THE GOSPEL ACCORDING TO DISNEY

Christian Values in the
Early Animated Classics

Philip Longfellow Anderson

***Foreword by Legendary Disney Animators
Frank Thomas and Ollie Johnston***

Longfellow Publishing
1999

The Gospel According to Disney: Christian Values in the Early Animated Classics

by Philip Longfellow Anderson

Published by:
Longfellow Publishing
P.O. Box 312
La Canada, California 91012-0312
http://www:longfellowpublishing.com

Cover Art: John Ballowe
Anderson, Philip Longfellow
The Gospel according to Disney: Christian values in the early animated classics / Philip Longfellow Anderson. —1st ed.
p. cm.
Includes bibliographical references.
LCCN: 98-97013
ISBN: 0-9669564-0-0

1. Motion pictures--Religious aspects--Christianity. 2. Motion pictures--Moral and ethical aspects. 3. Walt Disney Productions--Miscellanea. 4. Christian ethics. I. Title.

PN1995.9.R4A53 1999 791.43'682
QBI99-90

Contents

"Greater love hath no one than he who lays down
his life for his friend."

Bagheera the panther
The Jungle Book

"No one has greater love than this, to lay down
one's life for one's friends."

Jesus of Nazareth
The Gospel According to John 15:13

ACKNOWLEDGMENT

The Author wishes to acknowledge the assistance and inspiration provided by the following people: Pat Anderson, Michael and Akiko Anderson, Phil and Katherine Markgraf, Heather Anderson, James and Catherine Morley, Marilyn Smith, Robert Anderson, Mike George, Nelson Meacham, Jeannie Pool, John Ballowe, Lynne Poole, Ollie and Marie Johnston, Frank and Jeanette Thomas, the congregations of Church of the Lighted Window (La Canada, California), The Community Church (Sebastopol, California), and The Community Church (Warden, Washington).

FOREWORD

by Frank Thomas and Ollie Johnston

Would you attend a worship service when the Minister's sermon was entitled one of the following?

POISON APPLES
Snow White And The Seven Dwarfs
Genesis 3:1-7

or

BECOMING A REAL HUMAN BEING
Pinocchio
Hebrews 4:12-13

Maybe the Minister got the publicity for his sermon mixed up with a United Artists Theater advertisement. It certainly sounds more like the Grimm Brothers or Walt Disney than Genesis or Hebrews. However, if you did decide to attend either service, you might be pleasantly surprised as well as stimulated with a different perspective, and perhaps a better way of looking at life.

Philip Longfellow Anderson has chosen problems and decisions faced by Disney characters, such as Pinocchio, and related them to the everyday difficulties we all run into. Often he has been able to do it with a humorous anecdote.

His thorough knowledge and understanding of the personalities in these pictures allows him to make honest and entertaining analogies which strengthen the lesson. This combined with his fine knowledge of the Bible makes for interesting reading and for listening, too.

Perhaps it was Walt Disney's great talent for having the

good triumph over evil through fantasy, magic and music that attracted Philip Anderson to our pictures. Altogether, he has found inspiration for twenty sermons based on Disney animated films. That represents barely half of the Studio's animated feature output, so we feel that Rev. Mr. Anderson still has enough material to give many more great sermons and write many more interesting books. We hope he does.

Frank Thomas Ollie Johnston

INTRODUCTION

A recent donation from Roy E. Disney to the Walt Disney Archives in Burbank, California is a Certificate of Baptism dated June 8, 1902. It is signed by W. R. Parr, the pastor of St. Paul Congregational Church, which was located in the northwestern part of Chicago, Illinois. The six-month-old baby boy being baptized was the fourth son of Elias and Flora Disney.

Elias was skilled as a carpenter. For the grand salary of one dollar a day, he had worked at the World's Columbian Exposition in Chicago—the historic observance of the 400th anniversary of Christopher Columbus' famous journey. So when St. Paul Congregational needed a new sanctuary, it was Elias who volunteered to build the building. He put up a plain, serviceable structure with a tall, sloping roof. Flora played the organ in the new church.

Elias was such a good friend of the minister that he even preached the sermons for him when the pastor was on vacation. It happened that both of their wives became pregnant in 1901. Elias made a proposal to the pastor: "Tell you what. If we have a boy, we'll name him after you. And if you have a boy, you name him after me." The Reverend Walter Parr thought this was a great idea. It turned out that both babies were boys. So the Parr family welcomed little Elias Parr into the parsonage. And, reciprocally, when their own baby was born on December 8, 1901 (that baby who was baptized six months later), the carpenter's family bestowed the name of their Congregational minister on their fourth child: Walter Elias Disney.

Having been baptized myself in a Congregational church (and serving as a pastor in churches of its successor denomination, the United Church of Christ), I take special delight in sharing this initial spiritual kinship with a man who, together with his brother Roy, embodied the driving force of a creative empire that in no small way has impacted the memory, language, and culture of the twentieth century and, no doubt, centuries to come.

Like countless people on this planet, many of my earliest impressions and values were influenced by something Disney—primarily the images and characters of the animated classics. Indeed, my appreciation for this influence has continued to expand as I have added years to my life.

Two thousand years ago Jesus of Nazareth used allegories, anecdotes, and illustrations to teach about the kingdom of God. He communicated his gospel more often through stories than sermons. A prodigal son reunited with a forgiving father.....a shepherd in search of a lost sheep.....a Samaritan showing sympathy to a victimized stranger: these parables have conveyed more levels of truth that I, or any pastor, could match in a hundred books or sermons.

So, too, I believe, there are many valuable lessons to be learned in the Disney animated classics. The loss of innocence, the cost of righteousness, vanity leading to disaster, sacrifice leading to resurrection—such are the recurring themes in these films. No, of course, they were not intended to be polemic. Nor are they exclusively relevant to one faith community and not to another. They are essentially entertainment, and sublimely successful in that endeavor. But, as with all unforgettable forms of art, a large measure of their success is the unique way in which they are able to communicate empathy and insight. For me, they have been a rich vein of material to be mined homiletically.

In an age when the media, for good or ill, play an increasingly potent role in shaping the value systems of human society, we can be grateful indeed for entertainment as humane and piquant as the Disney animated features.

The first "Disney sermon" I ever preached happened to be prompted by a friendship with Clarence Nash, the voice of Donald Duck for half a century. When I shared from the pulpit the original version of the final chapter in this volume (*The Temper of Donald Duck*), Clarence sat in the front pew and answered questions from the congregation following the service.

The enduring impact of the early animated classics can be attributed to a fortuitous combination of talents. Primary among them were the "Nine Old Men," nine exceptionally creative artists Walt Disney hired in the early years of the studio.

It has been my good fortune in recent years to include among my friends two of these incomparable pioneers, Frank Thomas and Ollie Johnston. Together they have created innumerable animated characters and scenes that have touched the emotions and imaginations of millions of human beings. They have also collaborated on a series of widely-acclaimed books in their unique field of expertise.

Frank and Ollie have been life-long friends and neighbors of one another, as well as professional colleagues. How grateful I am to them for their wise counsel, for being present when several of these chapters were first preached as sermons, and for giving the world a legacy that defies measurement.

The chapters in this volume include all the animated features produced during Walt Disney's own lifetime, from *Snow White and The Seven Dwarfs* to *The Jungle Book*. Because the Disney studios continue to produce modern "classics", it is my hope to include them in another volume.

Each chapter concludes with a few general questions. The individual reader is encouraged to consider them. Families who enjoy watching and re-watching these films from their own video libraries might wish to use such questions to stimulate family discussion. Study groups and youth fellowships may choose to employ them in a Christian Education program.

May you, the reader of this book, go far beyond my fallible musings to deepen your own faith in the Lord whose gospel animates every moment of life with promise and glory.

CHAPTER 1:

POISON APPLES: *SNOW WHITE AND THE SEVEN DWARFS*

Now the serpent was more crafty than any other wild animal that the Lord God had made. He said to the woman, "Did God say, 'You shall not eat from any tree in the garden'?" The woman said to the serpent, "We may eat of the fruit of the trees in the garden; but God said, 'You shall not eat of the fruit of the tree that is in the middle of the garden, nor shall you touch it, or you shall die.'" But the serpent said to the woman, "You will not die; for God knows that when you eat of it your eyes will be opened, and you will be like God, knowing good and evil." So when the woman saw that the tree was good for food, and that it was a delight to the eyes, and that the tree was to be desired to make one wise, she took of its fruit and ate; and she also gave some to her husband, who was with her, and he ate. Then the eyes of both were opened, and they knew that they were naked; and they sewed fig leaves together and made loincloths for themselves.

Genesis 3:1-7

Snow White and The Seven Dwarfs was a milestone in motion picture history. It was the first full-length animated feature and an affirmation of the preeminence of the Walt Disney studios in this unique and emerging art form. It was an unqualified success—commercially and critically—and continues to be the touchstone by which successive animated features are invariably compared.

This Disney version of the old Grimm's fairy tale introduced characters and songs that are still beloved by millions of people around the world. Yet, typically, for perfectionist Walt Disney himself it represented only a beginning. As he told reporter Paul Harrison at the time of its release, "I am conscious only of the places where it could be improved. You see, we've learned such a lot since we started this thing, I wish I could yank it back and do it all over again." [1]

As anyone already familiar with the story knows, a key element in the plot is a poison apple—an apple that the villain uses in her attempt to destroy the heroine. Indeed, without the apple and the danger it represents, the story would probably limp into atrophy. The apple lends the drama its meaning and its urgency.

The same is true of another old story—one that's even older than *Snow White and The Seven Dwarfs.* It is found in the first book of the Bible, Genesis. It's the story of the man and the woman—called Adam and Eve in Hebrew—in the Garden of Eden. However, we must be fair and note that the Bible never specifically mentions an apple. It might have been an orange, or a kumquat, or a persimmon. Nevertheless, legend and tradition have combined to produce this popular misconception of identifying it as an apple. I wouldn't be surprised if the Brothers Grimm themselves had this Eden "apple" in mind when they first related the story of *Snow White.*

So perhaps it's not out of line to make some comparisons between the Disney classic and this Old Testament narrative that represents an archetype of the human condition. And to do so, let's focus on those "apples"—those poison apples.

<u>First</u> of all, consider the <u>poisoners</u>—the promoters of the

apples. The very first character ever to appear in a Disney feature film is a Queen. She is wearing a golden crown and a purple-black robe. Her features are icily attractive, but we can sense a coldbloodedness beneath her beauty. She is obsessed with her own appearance. She regularly consults her magic mirror to ask, "Who is the fairest of them all?" It is that fateful day when the mirror answers with the name of Snow White wherein the Queen reveals the cruel extent of the evil within her own soul.

Snow White, as the opening narrative informs us, is the Queen's stepdaughter, the Princess. The Queen has long been afraid that the girl's beauty would some day exceed her own. So she has dressed Snow White in rags and treated her as a Scullery Maid. We first see Snow White singing beside a well. Her lovely voice attracts a passing Prince, who hops over the castle wall to join her. She demurely retreats into the castle. The Prince proceeds to serenade her with a love song.

The Queen observes the scene with furious displeasure. It clearly confirms the judgment of the mirror that Snow White has become the fairest in the land. The Queen orders her huntsman to take Snow White into the forest and kill her. He is reluctant to carry out such a terrible task. But the Queen threatens him with dire consequences if he refuses. She even demands that he bring back Snow White's heart in a box as proof of the girl's demise.

Once they are in the forest, the huntsman raises his knife to slay the Princess. But he finds that he is unable to carry out this vicious plan. Instead, he warns Snow White to flee from the Queen's jealousy. In her panic, Snow White runs further into the forest. With the coming of night every tree and branch seems like a monster in a nightmare.

When daytime returns, Snow White finds herself in the company of friendly animals, who then guide her to a cottage where seven dwarfs are the residents. Through some delightful scenes of discovery and introduction, they all soon become like a family.

But, through the magic of her mirror, the Queen discovers that Snow White is still alive. The huntsman has brought her the heart of a pig instead of a princess. So, in her vanity and her jealousy and her rage, the Queen transforms herself into an old hag, a witch, and produces a poison apple, by which she intends to destroy Snow White.

In the Genesis story the poisoner is a serpent—associated elsewhere throughout the Bible with Satan, the Devil, the Tempter, the personification of evil. In Genesis the serpent is identified as being "more crafty than any other wild animal that the Lord God had made." *(Genesis 3:1).* He is jealous of the Creator, and deceptive in his attempt to invert the balances of creation itself.

Genesis begins with the story of creation itself—how God brought forth order from chaos, light from darkness, and how God created living creatures to populate the earth. The climax of the story is the creation of humankind. "So God created humankind in his image, in the image of God he created them; male and female he created them." *(Genesis 1:27)*

So the man and woman find themselves living in the Garden of Eden with only one restriction: They are not to eat the fruit of one particular tree. There is something poison about this "apple".

But then they encounter the serpent, the craftiest of all the creatures in creation. Like the evil Queen in *Snow White and The Seven Dwarfs*, the serpent is willing to deceive, poison, and destroy the innocent for his own selfish ends.

Surely we don't have to turn many pages of this morning's newspaper to find ample evidence of such poisoners in our midst today. From the profiteer who sells illegal drugs, to the charlatan who perverts gullible minds, to the hate group that preaches bigotry—there's no shortage of poisoners in our neighborhoods. And sometimes they can be as certified as a Queen.

There's an old New England saying that when the devil goes to church, he sits in the choir. The true poisoners of society are not always the scuzzy and the scandalous. They may sit at the tables of power and play the games of guile. Some of them are even oblivious to the toxic consequences of their vanity.

J.B. Priestley's play, *An Inspector Calls*, tells of a police inspector who calls upon a respectable, prosperous family to inform them that a desperate young woman has committed suicide. He'd like to ask each of them a few questions. "It has nothing to do with us," they protest. But when each of them sees her picture, each one recognizes it. The father remembers he had fired her from his factory because she had asked for another half-dollar a week. The daughter recognizes her as a dress shop assistant about whom she had complained in a fit of bad temper, and who had been dismissed as a result. One by one—the merchant, his daughter, his wife, his prospective son-in-law—they have all injected the poisons of rejection, indifference and despair into the life of this young woman, and driven her into the despair that destroyed her.

Some of the greatest crimes in history have been committed, not by disreputable dissenters, but by outwardly respectable people—driven by emotions such as envy and jealousy and greed.

Cornelius Vanderbilt, who controlled the mighty New York Central Railroad, looked with contempt upon Jay Gould, who headed the smaller Erie Railroad. He determined he was going to put Gould out of the railroad business. In those days cattle were being shipped from the west to Buffalo, and then re-shipped to New York City over one of these two lines. The prevailing rate for a carload of cattle was $100. Vanderbilt cut the price to $75. As anticipated, Gould reduced it to $50. Vanderbilt went to $25. Gould made it $10. Determined to ruin his competitor, Vanderbilt slashed the price to $1 a carload. That was enough for Gould. He refused to meet this last price, and the business went to the New York Central. Although it had been expensive, Vanderbilt felt that it had been worth the cost to bring Gould to his knees.

However, the triumph was short-lived. After a few weeks had passed, he learned that Gould had bought all the cattle coming into Buffalo and had shipped them to New York City via the Central at $1 a carload, cleaning up a fortune at Vanderbilt's expense. [2]

In the balances of destiny, poisoners often become the victims of their own venom. An old Hindu story tells of a two-headed bird that began quarreling. When one head wasn't looking, the other head dropped some poison into its food, which was soon eaten. The murderous head then began chuckling quietly to itself. But not for long. In a few minutes the chuckling ceased, for the poison had gone to a common stomach, and neither head could survive.

Life is forever endangered by its poisoners.

Consider now, in the <u>second</u> place, the <u>poison apples</u> themselves in our stories. One of the things they have in common is their fraudulence. They don't look like poison. Quite the opposite! They look like the most attractive of all fruits. They promise something wonderful, yet they deliver something dreadful.

Snow White is alone in the dwarfs' cottage, baking them a gooseberry pie, when the Queen, disguised as an old hag, appears with the poison apple. Feigning heart problems, she persuades Snow White to invite her inside the cottage, where she pretends to reward Snow White by offering her a bite of the apple. "It's a magic wishing apple," she promises. "One bite, and all your dreams come true."

That's a temptation Snow White has difficulty ignoring. After all, earlier in the story Snow White had met a handsome Prince. She dreams of him carrying her off to his castle, and living happily ever after. If the bite of an apple can give her this god-like power—if it can make her this omnipotent—why not consume it? So she yields to the temptation of the Queen's false promise. She tastes the apple and becomes the victim of the poison's curse. She drops to the floor in a death-like coma.

In the Genesis story the woman receives a similar promise from the serpent. When she tells the serpent that God has given them access to all the fruit except for a single tree, the serpent tempts her to taste the fruit of that one tree. The serpent says to her, fang-in-cheek, that God doesn't want them to eat from it because—in the words Genesis ascribes to this talking reptile—"you will be like God, knowing good and evil" *(Genesis 3:5)*. So the woman, Eve, not only eats the fruit, she also persuades the man, Adam, to do the same.

However, the consequence is not salvation, but shame. Instead of becoming more like God, they are abruptly and mortifyingly confronted with the truth of how unlike God they really are. They suddenly see their own nakedness, a biblical metaphor for humiliation. They are expelled from the Garden. Their days are numbered and exposed to the hardest edges of life—pain, toil, the fratricide of their son Abel by another son, Cain. The fruit they had desired has become poison in their mouths.

Clare Booth Luce served for a time as United States Ambassador to Italy. She established her residence in a beautiful seventeenth-century Italian villa. In particular, she loved the bedroom and its ceiling, ornately decorated with beautiful designs of roses in bas relief. Some months after moving into her new home, she began to notice that she was deteriorating physically. She was tired. She lost weight. She had little energy. It was finally determined at the American Naval Hospital that she was suffering from arsenic poisoning. Everyone on her staff received extensive security checks, but there seemed no possibility that anyone was trying to do away with her. According to Luce, they finally discovered the cause of the poisoning. Those beautiful roses on her bedroom ceiling had been painted with a paint that contained arsenic lead. A fine dust would fall from those roses onto the bed where Mrs. Luce would be sleeping or looking up to admire them. As beautiful as they appeared, they were in reality a deadly poison.

So it is that some of the things that seem to us so attractive may be the very things that defile us and threaten to destroy us. An addictive drug, an illicit romance, an act of vengeance, an uncontrolled passion, a selfish temptation—they may promise bliss, yet deliver tragedy. How easily we can be seduced by the deceptive.

A fellow woke up one morning with the feeling that something different was going to happen that day. He glanced out the window at the thermometer. It read 33 degrees. He went downstairs. Strangely, the clock had stopped at 3 o'clock. He picked up the morning paper and noticed the date: the third of the month. On a hunch, he looked at the third page of the third section. Sure enough, it was the racing section. In the third race, one of the entries was a horse named Trio! The fellow couldn't wait to get to the bank. He drew out his life savings, and bet it all on Trio to win that race. Trio came in third!

Some promises can seem so alluring—some fruit so attractive—that we put aside the logic of everything else we know to be true in order to pursue that promise. What tragedies we crash into when we find the promise itself is poison.

The Genesis story is sometimes called the original story of

sin, or the story of the "original sin". In any event, it identifies a poison apple that can seduce even the most innocent of us. Eat this fruit—promises the serpent—and you will be like God. Therein lies the essential nature of sin: the rejection of the role God created for us in the universe—seeking instead to put ourselves at its center, coveting for ourselves the place that belongs to God alone. God alone is the divine Creator. God alone defines good and evil. God alone has the power to make all dreams come true.

If only Snow White had remembered that—and had not been deceived by a poisoned promise that she could have anything her heart desired.....the fraudulent promise that she could do what God alone can do if only she would trust a stranger's word and an apple's charm! Yet whatever a poison apple may promise, it has nothing to deliver but its own lethal poison.

But, now, there's a <u>third</u> thing to be said about these poison apples. <u>They are not without an antidote</u>. There is a remedy to redeem their curse.

For Snow White, it's the healing power of love's first kiss. In one of animation's first, and most memorable, scenes to convey a powerful emotional impact—Snow White is depicted in her death-like sleep, surrounded by the seven dwarfs, who mourn her apparent demise. The poignancy of their grief testifies to the depth of their love for her.

As they weep together, the Prince, who had captured Snow White's heart early in the story, enters the scene. And although he, too, must believe her to be dead, he cannot help but approach Snow White and express his love with a kiss. And that kiss—that expression of love—overcomes all the evil that the poison apple has produced. And Snow White is released from her sleep and returned to the realm of life. The closing titles of the film assure us that they lived happily ever after.

The story of Eden is no less redemptive. For the God who is the God of justice and judgment—who validates life with law, and who links law with consequence—is also a God of love. God's ultimate purpose for us is not poison but compassion.

The raw world into which the man and the woman—you and I—are thrust is indeed a world where a human being can never become God. But it is a world in which God has chosen to become human. That's the gospel the Christian Church celebrates today and every day. That's why it calls Jesus the Christ.....not because he was some lucky human being who found a key to divinity, but because his life reveals a God who joins us in our humanity.

In Christ we discover that salvation is not some magic fruit to ingest into our lives for selfish satisfaction. Rather, it is a love that already surrounds us wherever we are—and a love that seeks to use us whoever we are.

Many years ago a young physician, Dr. Claude Barlow, went to Shaohing, China, as a medical missionary. In working with the people, he soon became aware of a disease that was taking the lives of a great many people. It was an unknown disease, with no known remedy. It wasn't described in any of the medical books. There was no laboratory equipment for research work in Shaohing. Yet Claude Barlow cared about these people who were being poisoned. He decided upon a daring procedure. He studied case after case of those infected. He filled his notebook with observations about the symptoms and the progress of the disease.

Then he boarded a ship for America, carrying with him a small vial containing germs of the disease. Just before he left the ship in New York harbor, Claude Barlow took these germs into his own body. Then, as quickly as he could, he made his way to the Johns Hopkins hospital, where he had studied.

He was already quite sick when he arrived, but he presented himself to his former professors as a human "guinea pig" for their study and experimentation. By the grace of God, they were successful. And when Claude Barlow returned to China, he took with him the antidote to treat and control this terrible disease that was poisoning the people he loved.

So, too, has the Son of God given himself for you and me. This is the gospel, the story of the depths of the love by which God embraces each of us. May we receive that love as an antidote for all the guilt and fear and reticence that poisons our lives and relationships. May we receive it—not as a magic potion to fulfill all our dreams, or to make us gods—but as a creative catalyst for compassion in the story of our own lives.

SOME QUESTIONS TO CONSIDER

1. Who are the most dangerous "poisoners" in our society today?
2. Can we find any clues on the outside to tell us what a person is like on the inside?
3. Why do you suppose God created the serpent?
4. Should Snow White have known not to eat the apple?
5. Is there ever a time or place for "playing God"?
6. What healing "kiss" (expression of love) do you need most right now?

CHAPTER 2:

BECOMING A REAL HUMAN BEING: *PINOCCHIO*

Indeed, the word of God is living and active, sharper than any two-edged sword, piercing until it divides soul from spirit, joints from marrow; it is able to judge the thoughts and intentions of the heart. And before him no creature is hidden, but all are naked and laid bare to the eyes of the one to whom we must render an account.

Hebrews 4:12-13

Walt Disney's *Pinocchio* was the studio's second animated feature, released about two years after the phenomenal success of *Snow White and The Seven Dwarfs.* The story of *Pinocchio* was based on a serialized nineteenth-century story by Carlo Lorenzini, whose pen name was Collodi.

Although Disney's *Pinocchio* was a commercial disappointment on its initial release, many critics have come to consider it not only technically superior to its predecessor, but perhaps the finest animated feature ever produced.

The title character in the film is a marionette who has been created by the kindly puppet-maker, Geppetto. Pinocchio is introduced in a delightful sequence wherein Geppetto manipulates his strings to make him walk. He teases the household kitten named Figaro, to the delight of the pet goldfish named Cleo.

That night, before Geppetto falls asleep, the puppet-maker wishes upon the Wishing Star that his marionette will become a real boy. As he sleeps, his wish is partially granted. The angelic Blue Fairy descends from the skies and grants the puppet the gift of life. Furthermore, she promises him that if he proves brave, truthful, and unselfish, he may one day indeed become a real boy.

A visiting cricket named Jiminy appears on the scene to give Pinocchio some advice, and, before the Blue Fairy disappears, she appoints him to be Pinocchio's conscience. Pinocchio and Jiminy begin to dance and sing together, and the noise awakens Geppetto, who is ecstatic to discover that his wooden creation has been given the gift of life. It's as if now he has a son.

The next morning Geppetto sends Pinocchio off to school. But Pinocchio is barely a few blocks from home when he is spotted by an unscrupulous fox named J. Worthington Foulfellow and his lackey, a cat named Gideon. They realize that Pinocchio represents an opportunity to make a fast buck. A walking, talking puppet is a novelty people would pay to see. So they convince Pinocchio that he should become an actor. Jiminy Cricket intervenes and tries to persuade Pinocchio that this is a temptation that can only have dire consequences. But Pinocchio is easily distracted, and the fox and the cat proceed to sell him to a traveling puppeteer named Stromboli.

One of animation history's most delightful and memorable scenes is Pinocchio's debut with the Stromboli troupe. Dancing variously with French, Dutch, and Russian marionettes who are being manipulated with strings, Pinocchio sings his signature song, "I've got no strings to hold me down, to make me fret or make me frown." The number ends with Pinocchio spinning wildly into the other puppets, so that he lands on the stage tangled in a veritable web of marionette strings just as he sings, ironically, his final line: "There are no strings on me!"

And here, I think, we encounter <u>one</u> of the great lessons of the story—one that Pinocchio must learn. <u>There *are* strings attached to life</u>. Even though he may be free from the strings by which a puppeteer manipulates a marionette, Pinocchio is not free from the strings of cause and effect, temptation and tragedy, responsibility and accountability, that are attached to all our decisions and remain inescapable conditions of being alive.

Pinocchio learns this woefully, following the performance, when he announces to Stromboli that he is about to return home. Stromboli responds with a wicked laugh and tells Pinocchio he has no intention of ever allowing the puppet to leave his troupe. He proceeds to lock Pinocchio in a bird-cage. Stromboli even threatens to chop Pinocchio into fire-wood if and when he's no longer useful to the puppeteer.

It's a cruel and shocking lesson.....a rude awakening for an innocent puppet who had allowed the voice of temptation to drown out the voice of his conscience telling him to go to school.

There are strings attached to life. We live in a moral universe where, ultimately, every one of us, in one way or another, is held accountable for what we are and what we do. As the New Testament Letter to the Hebrews says of God: "Before him no creature is hidden, but all are naked and laid bare to the eyes of the one to whom we must render an account" *(Hebrews 4:13)*. We cannot escape—and must eventually face up to—the consequences of our decisions and actions.

A little boy named Charlie was busy picking up the toys which he'd scattered around the house. The visiting pastor commended him for it and inquired with a smile, "Did your mother promise you something for picking them up?" Charlie replied, "No, sir, but she promised me something if I didn't." There are strings attached to all our decisions and actions. We ignore that lesson to our own peril.

The story is told of a $500 bounty offered for wolves captured alive. It turned Joe and Charlie into fortune hunters. Day and night they searched the mountains and forests looking for their valuable prey. Exhausted one night, they fell asleep dreaming of their potential fortune. Suddenly, Joe awoke to see that they were surrounded by about fifty wolves with flaming eyes and bared teeth. He nudged his friend and said, "Charlie, wake up! We're rich!"

It's an old cliche: Be careful what you look for, ask for, pray for. You might get it! Whenever we pull on one end of a string, we're causing something to happen at the other end. When we heed the voice of temptation rather than the voice of conscience, we may even be tying strings around our own neck.

A magazine writer reported shortly after the Second World War finding a grave somewhere in France which had a marker with this inscription: "In memory of Maggie, a mule who kicked 1 colonel, 1 major, 3 lieutenants, 11 sergeants, 27 privates, and 1 bomb."

People's transgressions have a way of catching up with them. Some years ago in Chicago a man wearing a ski-mask brutally assaulted a woman outside of her apartment. It was the middle of summer. Police later arrested a man who fit the description. A search of the suspect's apartment yielded only one possible item of evidence: a ski mask just like the one worn by the assailant. Yet the man testified under oath that it hadn't been worn since the previous winter. With no other witnesses, a conviction was extremely doubtful. Then a University of Illinois entomologist was consulted to examine the evidence. The entomologist found a small cocklebur embedded in the mask, and inside the seed a tiny beetle just a few weeks old. The expert explained to the jury that this beetle could not have survived from a previous winter. Someone recently had worn the mask in the local vicinity of the assault scene, because the cocklebur came from a species common to that area. Confronted by the evidence, the defendant broke down and confessed.

No, our court system is not infallible. Nor are the scales of justice always balanced within a person's lifetime. Some of the world's saints die in poverty and disgrace, while some of the most despicable people around get praised at their funerals. But ultimately—whether in this life or beyond it—we are indeed held accountable for what we are and do.

Some years ago a master counterfeiter, after a long and painstaking effort, finally believed that he had achieved the perfect copy of a twenty-dollar bill. But in spite of every precaution, he was soon apprehended by a treasury agent. He was so confident in his foolproof engravings that he defied the agent to find any difference—however minute—between the counterfeit bill and the bill from which it had been copied. To his astonishment, the treasury agent replied: "I can find no difference. That's the trouble. You made only one mistake. The bill from which you copied your counterfeit was *itself* a counterfeit!"

That's the tragedy of so many lives. Their hopes and values are modeled after something counterfeit—something false—something at cross purposes with the truth at the heart of the universe itself.

The historian James Anthony Froude, at the end of a lifetime spent in the study of human history, came to this conclusion: "One lesson and only one, history may be said to repeat with distinctiveness: that the world is built somehow on moral foundations; that in the long run it is well with the good; in the long run it is ill with the wicked."

So there was Pinocchio locked in a bird cage in Stromboli's wagon—having come face to face with the sobering lesson of accountability. There are strings attached to life. If we yield to temptation, we'd better be prepared to face the consequences.

As Stromboli's wagon rolls out of town, Pinocchio's appointed conscience, Jiminy Cricket, hops aboard, just to say farewell to his friend. When he discovers Pinocchio's plight, he does everything a cricket can do to release the puppet. But, unfortunately, that doesn't prove to be much.

Then, just when everything seems lost, help comes from above. The Blue Fairy appears in the wagon and begins to question Pinocchio about his predicament. Pinocchio starts making excuses for himself, telling lies about the reasons for his incarceration. And with each successive untruth, Pinocchio's wooden nose grows longer and longer. Finally it becomes a veritable tree branch, complete with leaves and a nest of birds on the end of it.

And here Pinocchio learns a <u>second</u> important lesson. As the Blue Fairy tells him, <u>"A lie keeps growing and growing until it's as plain as the nose on your face."</u> There is a disfiguring quality about dishonesty.

A lie can become as plain as the nose on your face. A twenty-five year old man was charged with the crime of robbing a number of vending machines. He protested his innocence, but police were interested to note that he posted his entire $400 bail using only nickels, dimes, and quarters.

In their book, *Supreme Folly*, Rodney Jones and Gerald Uelmen tell of a woman in Oroville, California, who eagerly attended a "Neighborhood Watch" meeting in her neighborhood. She was particularly interested in the program, because a storage locker she rented had recently been broken into, and her television set, Christmas stockings, and a favorite dress had been stolen. While two police officers made their presentation, this woman looked around at the home of her neighbor where the meeting was being held. To her astonishment, her own TV was in the corner, her Christmas stockings were hung by the fireplace, and the hostess was wearing her dress! Following the meeting, she informed the officers, who later returned with a search warrant. The "Neighborhood Watch" host and hostess were arrested when thousands of dollars worth of stolen property was discovered in the house. [3]

A lie can become as plain as the nose on your face. Yet that doesn't seem to discourage the practice. A conversation is reported to have taken place recently between two Hollywood executives at breakfast in a hotel. There was a point at which one of them raised his voice and declared, "You're lying to me!" The other executive nodded and replied, "I know. You're right. But hear me out."

We've almost gotten to the point where we take for granted that some people are lying: when they're trying to sell us something, when they're bragging at a high school reunion, when they're running for political office. Some commentator has said we've come a long way in 200 years. George Washington couldn't tell a lie—but today, we have thousands of politicians who can. There's been a kind of disfiguring disenchantment in recent years with those who hold political office. It's not that politicians a century ago were scrupulously honest and altogether free from corruption. But public attention and media exposure today have combined to shine spotlights into corners that previously remained in the darkness. From Watergate to this morning's newspaper, the hottest political news stories of the last few decades seem to illustrate the lesson: A lie can become as plain as the nose on your face.

The ancient Chinese had an unusual approach for determining dishonesty—a kind of lie detector test. Apparently they knew that fear inhibits the production of saliva in most people. So, if someone were accused of being dishonest, that person would be given a handful of rice to chew. If that person could spit it out, he was declared to be telling the truth. But if he couldn't produce enough saliva to do this, he was judged to be afraid of being discovered, and therefore guilty of lying.

However a person may pass or flunk the "saliva" test, and however apparently a lie may disfigure an individual's public image or reputation, there is no way anyone can ever disguise dishonesty before God. Again, in the words of Hebrews, "Before him no creature is hidden, but all are naked and laid bare to the eyes of the one to whom we must render an account" *(Hebrews 4:13)*. To God, even if to no one else, a lie is as plain as the nose on your face.

When Pinocchio learns this important lesson, and promises not to lie again, the Blue Fairy restores his appearance and unlocks the cage where he is a prisoner. The story continues to unfold with additional twists and turns. J. Worthington Foulfellow and Gideon deliver Pinocchio to a Coachman who eventually takes the puppet to Pleasure Island, a realm of boyhood self-indulgence. As it turns out, self-indulgence on Pleasure Island turns real boys into something less than human—into jackasses, whom the Coachman proceeds to consign to such fates as labor in the the salt mines. Before Pinocchio succumbs completely to this animalization, he is able to escape from the Island—but not before acquiring a donkey's ears and tail.

His destination is home. But when he and Jiminy finally get there, the home is empty. In their moment of despair, a message is brought to them by a dove revealing that Geppetto—who has been searching for Pinocchio—is aboard an old wreck of a ship that has been swallowed by Monstro, the largest and most ferocious whale in the ocean.

When he learns this, there is a profound change in Pinocchio. His only thought is that he must save the man who has become his father. Without a thought for his own safety and well-being, he bravely jumps into the sea with a rock tied to his tail to take him to the bottom. Then he engages in an underwater quest to find Geppetto. He finally succeeds when he, too, is swallowed by the same whale. There's a glorious reunion, followed by the sober realization that few things that go into a whale get out alive.

But, in the tradition of the Old Testament prophet Jonah, Pinocchio's story doesn't end inside "the belly of the fish" *(Jonah 1:17)*. The puppet gets an idea. He builds a fire aboard their ship which produces smoke that causes the whale to sneeze—thereby ejecting all the characters aboard the ship. The sneeze infuriates the whale who tries to destroy them all. Floundering in the water, Geppetto tells Pinocchio to swim for shore and save himself. But in an act of courageous unselfishness, Pinocchio refuses to leave the puppet maker and risks his own life to bring him to safety. After a frantic chase that ends with the whale crashing into the rocky cliffs bordering the sea, everyone is safely accounted for.....everyone, that is, except for Pinocchio, who is lying motionless, face down in a pool of water in the sand. He had been willing to give up his life for the sake of his father.

Back at home, the little family of characters gathers around the body of Pinocchio to mourn. But then, miraculously, the voice of the Blue Fairy is heard once again—and the scene suddenly becomes one of resurrection. Pinocchio not only returns to life, but he no longer has the complexion of wood and paint, because he has indeed become a real boy.

He has learned a <u>third</u> lesson—one that has finally transformed him from a wooden puppet into a real human being. <u>He has proven himself unselfish</u>. He has been willing even to sacrifice his own life for someone else.

And here, perhaps, is the most important insight of this story for us. For if you and I are also to be human, really human—human in the sense for which God created us—we, too, must learn these lessons that Pinocchio learned: bravery, truthfulness and, above all, the lesson of unselfishness.

Earlier this century the congregation of a downtown church in Chicago rented the Iroquois Theatre to use on Sundays for worship while the church sanctuary was being redecorated. The pastor, Frank Gonzales, had a nephew named Will, who was attending Northwestern University. Will was a fullback on the football team. Will dropped by his uncle's study one Saturday afternoon, and the pastor asked Will if he wouldn't mind taking the church bulletins over to the theatre to leave them in the office for the next morning's service. Will was happy to oblige.

As Will approached the theatre, he could see wisps of smoke coming out of the roof. It was the matinee performance of a new production, and the theatre was packed with people. Will could hear pandemonium breaking out inside the theatre as the audience became aware of the fire.

Will dropped the bulletins and ran into the building and onto the stage. It was a scene of mass hysteria. People were scrambling to find an exit. As he looked up, it became apparent that no one was moving on the third balcony. He ran up the stairs and found all the people backed up against an exit door that was stuck. With all the power of his fullback training, he smashed against the door repeatedly, and was finally able to get it open.

But then when he stepped out onto the fire escape, he discovered there was no fire escape ladder. By now smoke was pouring up the internal stairways, so something had to be done quickly. Looking around, Will spotted a piece of scaffolding that had been discarded. It was barely long enough to reach the edge of the next building. So Will braced himself to help every person cross the plank to safety. Some urged him to go ahead himself, but he didn't budge until every one else was across. By then flames had begun eating away at the plank. As he tried to walk across it alone, the plank lost its footing, and Will plunged three stories to the pavement below.

Will was barely conscious when his uncle arrived on the scene. The look of peace on his face radiated his satisfaction and gratitude that he had been able to help save lives that would otherwise have been lost. Will expired a few hours later from his injuries. For many years, one of the great treasures among the trophies at Northwestern University has been an old charred plank of wood with Will's name burned into it, a lasting testimonial to a young man who had proven himself brave, truthful and unselfish—a young man to whom many others knew they owed their lives.

A charred wooden plank—and a little wooden puppet—teach us lessons in what it means to become a real human being. And so, too, does an old wooden Cross embrace our human lives with an unselfish love that is eternal and divine.

SOME QUESTIONS TO CONSIDER

1. Are we finally accountable to anyone else besides God?
2. Can our conscience (our Jiminy Cricket) ever be wrong?
3. Are there occasions when a "little white lie" is harmless or acceptable?
4. Who is the most villainous character in *Pinocchio*: J. Worthington Foulfellow, Gideon, Stromboli, the Coachman, Monstro the Whale? Why?
5. In what sense is "being human" both a confession and a virtue?
6. Who is the most unselfish person you know?

CHAPTER 3:

LIFE'S MOST PERPLEXING QUESTION: *FANTASIA*

It was nine o'clock in the morning when they crucified him. The inscription of the charge against him read, "The King of the Jews." And with him they crucified two bandits, one on his right and one on his left. Those who passed by derided him, shaking their heads and saying, "Aha! You who would destroy the temple and build it in three days, save yourself, and come down from the cross!" In the same way the chief priests, along with the scribes, were also mocking him among themselves and saying, "He saved others; he cannot save himself. Let the Messiah, the King of Israel, come down from the cross now, so that we may see and believe." Those who were crucified with him also taunted him.

When it was noon, darkness came over the whole land until three in the afternoon. At three o'clock Jesus cried out with a loud voice, "Eloi, Eloi, lema sabachthani?" which means, "My God, my God, why have you forsaken me?"

Mark 15:25-34

In his first decade as a film star, Mickey Mouse graduated from black-and-white slapstick to full-color drama. Somewhere along the way Walt Disney got the idea of starring Mickey in the ancient story of "The Sorcerer's Apprentice." According to one report, Disney chanced to be having dinner one evening in a restaurant where the orchestra conductor Leopold Stokowski was dining alone. Disney invited Stokowski to join him at his table, and eventually proposed a collaboration on this project.

Further meetings and discussions convinced the two men to expand the idea, and to create a whole series of visualizations of musical themes. The result was the Disney Studio's third and most ambitious animated feature, *Fantasia*. It was intended to be much more than a movie. It was to be a reserved-seat-only concert presentation, with additional segments to be developed and added in years to come.

An innovative sound system was created, called "Fantasound," anticipating by a decade the advent of stereophonic recording. It involved as many as thirty-three different microphones strategically placed to record the orchestra, so that the theater audience would be surrounded by the music.

A number of prestigious theaters in major cities across the country were equipped with this audio system at a cost of thirty thousand dollars apiece. In addition, special lighting and curtain controls were installed, and theater employees were given special training in dealing with audiences courteously, as if they were attending a classical concert. Then on November 13, 1940, *Fantasia* had its world premiere at the Broadway Theater in New York, the same theater where Mickey Mouse had made his public debut as *Steamboat Willie* a dozen years earlier.

Today *Fantasia* has come to be regarded as a stunningly innovative film classic. It was one of the first twenty-five films chosen by the Library of Congress for its National Film Registry of significant motion pictures. The American Film Institute recently named it one of the hundred greatest American movies ever made. When it was released on video-tape, it broke all previous sales records.

But its initial release was a disaster. Many of those 1940

critics panned it, and the public response was, at best, lukewarm. Furthermore, war was escalating in Europe. Foreign markets were closed. So the bankers put pressure on Disney to abandon the expensive sound technology, cut thirty-nine minutes from its concert presentation format, and put it into general distribution as a double feature with a western. The consequence was a major financial loss for the Studio, and a heartbreak for all those involved.

It was one more evidence that life can sometimes seem dramatically unfair. Just when things ought to go right, they often go painfully wrong. Indeed, the adversities and tragedies of life turn many people into cynics.

For the person of faith, it remains life's most perplexing question: Why? If there is a God—and God is good and loving and powerful—why are there bad things in the world? In particular, why is there tragedy, and why do people suffer? It would seem that Jesus himself asked that question from the Cross: "My God, my God, why have you forsaken me?" *(Mark 27:46)* That cry has echoed across the centuries—and surely has emerged in some form from our own lips and hearts.

The only child born to a young couple carries an imperfect gene and must stumble blindly and painfully to an early grave. Why? A kindly old gentleman puts his foot on a slippery floor, and in a moment is permanently sentenced to bed for the rest of his life with a badly broken hip that won't heal. Why? A young soldier in the uniform of his country is struck down on a distant battlefield and left to die alone. Why?

Earthquakes and famines, wars and disease, and from the fallout come the cries of people in anguish. And we can't hear that sound without seeing before us a large question mark looming over all the suffering in life. Why? Why—if there is a God, and God is good and loving and powerful—why do people suffer?

Now, if we could accept the premise, as many have done, that there is no God.....that human life is essentially meaningless and godless.....then the problem of suffering goes away. Why shouldn't people suffer? There's nothing personal about the universe—no moral distinction between right and wrong, good and evil, pleasure and pain. What exists, is. No explanation of its meaning is either possible or even desirable.

But most of us are not so ready and willing to discard our religious faith. We see too much divinity in life to call it hopeless and meaningless. We witness too much rationality in human and natural relationships to call them irrational and absurd. We experience too much love and joy to call ourselves cosmic accidents. We appreciate too deeply the beauty of rosebuds and symphonies and faithful friends not to see in them some evidence of the love of God.

And that's why the question is so agonizingly real for us. If God truly loves us, why do people, even the best of people, suffer? This question is as pressing and relevant as this morning's headlines.

One idea we must dismiss immediately is the idea that God himself wants us, and causes us, to suffer. Since the days of Job's comforters and before, there have always been those who have argued that all suffering is the sign of God's disfavor—God's punishment for wrong-doing. Lyman Beecher, the noted nineteenth-century American preacher, preached a sermon one Sunday. It seems another church in his neighborhood had caught fire and burned to the ground. Beecher spent nearly an hour declaring it to be the righteous judgment of God on false doctrine. However, before the week was up, Beecher's own church burned down, too!

No, our understanding of God is primitive and inadequate, if we think of God causing suffering deliberately, inflicting it upon us willfully—like a monarch testing his subjects. Instead, let's honestly face up to the fundamental causes of tragedy and suffering. Every single one of them is a sign, not of a God who is capricious and doesn't care, but of a God who cares and loves us deeply. And perhaps *Fantasia* can help to illustrate this truth.

<u>One</u> of the causes of all suffering and tragedy is God's gift of <u>personal freedom</u>. Consider the story of "The Sorcerer's Apprentice"—set to the music of Paul Dukas—the tale that was the catalyst for *Fantasia*. It tells of a sorcerer's assistant, played by Mickey Mouse, who has the responsibility of hauling buckets of water from an outdoor fountain to fill an indoor reservoir. In the midst of his labors, he stops to watch in amazement as his boss exercises magical powers while wearing a cone-like wizard's hat. Soon the sorcerer retires, leaving his magical hat behind. Mickey—having a will of his own—freedom of choice—decides to try the hat on for himself, to dabble in some magic that might save himself a lot of toil. Without carefully considering all the consequences, he puts on the hat and transforms a broom into a living thing, which he commands to take over his water-hauling duties.

At first, it seems to work beautifully. The animated broom begins bringing water into the house. A satisfied Mickey soon falls asleep, and begins dreaming of god-like powers that may await him and his newly-discovered magic.

However, he is abruptly awakened when he finds himself waist-deep in water. The broom has over-performed. Mickey tries to use magic to stop the broom, but what he freely started, he is unable to stop. Finally he grabs an ax and chops the broom into splinters. But to his horror, each splinter becomes a new broom. Now he is surrounded by numerous water carriers, threatening to drown everything in sight. It's a calamity. Then, just when it almost seems too late, the sorcerer reappears. Assessing the situation, he immediately makes the water disappear. His magic does not require wearing the hat, which Mickey now sheepishly returns before returning to his duties, a chastened and humbler mouse.

Among God's greatest gifts to humanity is the gift of freedom. A human being has the power of choice. He or she is not a puppet, but a person. He can act according to his own decision, instead of according to divine compulsion. This is what introduces him to the whole dimension of morality—which is to say, it is better for him to do some things than to do other things.....to love, for instance, instead of to hate.

In order for human beings to have the freedom to choose what is right, they must also have the freedom to choose what is wrong—or there would be no freedom, no choice. And herein lies the cause of so much of the world's suffering and tragedy. I can misuse the gift I have been given. I can disrupt the way God has intended life to be lived. In theological terms, I can submit to the power of sin—the consequences of which always cause suffering. Because I have freedom, I can pat you on the back, or I can stab you in the back.

There's an ancient story of a cynic who wanted to outwit a wise old sage. He came to the sage with a tiny bird in his hand—a bird so small that he could conceal it entirely in his closed fist. "What do I have in my hand?" he asked. And the sage answered, "A bird." Now the cynic thought he had him: "And is the bird dead or alive?" It was his plan to trap the sage by letting the bird fly away if he answered "dead"—or by crushing the life out of it if he said "alive". He repeated the question, "Is it dead or alive?" In his wisdom, the sage simply said, "It is as you choose."

A major portion of the world's sufferings—from wars and murders to so many other kinds of physical and mental anguish—is caused by our power of choice. Our power of choice is our gift of personal freedom—that which makes us human beings instead of robots. Yet that same gift of freedom is one of the greatest signs that we are loved by God.

But, then, what about earthquakes and cancer and plane crashes—and all the other kinds of tragedies that don't seem to relate to human freedom?

Let's return to *Fantasia* and the segment based on Igor Stravinsky's composition, "Rite of Spring". The Disney artists chose to use this music to depict the dawn of the earth's creation. We graphically see the operation of natural laws that nurture life and destroy it, and bring forth new life. We first see the solar system and move closer to the earth, where we encounter volcanic craters sending rivers of lava to the sea. Then in the sea we begin to perceive tiny one-celled creatures, then more sophisticated life forms, fish, lungfish, amphibians. On the surface of the earth we begin to encounter pterodactyls and dinosaurs. We learn about the survival of the fittest as a Tyrannosaurus Rex appears and slays a Stegosaurus. Then we see the sun shining with such terrible heat that the sources of water dry up, and plant life virtually disappears. Migrating dinosaurs, denied their sustenance, begin to drop in their tracks. Some are trapped in tar pits. Soon only skeletons remain. Then an eclipse of the sun brings the dawn of a new era. The planet trembles with earthquakes that create mountains and valleys and tidal waves that wash the earth with water once again. This is an earth that is ruled by natural laws that will one day allow it to evolve into a home for human life.

Here is a <u>second</u> gift from God. <u>God has structured this universe according to certain dependable natural laws</u>, without which life would be utterly impossible. There are laws such as the law of gravity, thermonuclear laws, the laws of medical science, even moral laws. The more we discover about these laws, the more they work for us, unless we get into situations where they work against us.

The law of gravity, for instance, exists clearly for our benefit. One moment without it would send us all flying into space. And the more we know about it, the more new possibilities begin to emerge. It allows us to design airplanes to travel thousands of feet above the surface of the earth—but if something should malfunction, it may also cause an airplane to crash to the ground. It would not be because God wanted it to happen—but because there would be sheer chaos if every time a plane were in danger of crashing, God would suspend the law of gravity. If God's laws are to be dependable, God must remain faithful to them.

There's always more to learn about those laws. Earthquakes speak of the stresses and strains by which the earth maintains certain balances. The more we study them and the more we know about them, the closer we may come to predicting them and preparing for them, thereby avoiding human suffering—perhaps one day even harnessing the energy they release.

There are laws in medicine and genetics that—the more we know about them—the more we're in a position to produce healthier human beings. Never, however, should we expect to produce immortal organisms—because another dependable law ordains that the cycle of life on earth has to end before the fullness of an eternal life, independent of this earth, can begin.

We would be lost without dependable laws. In one of the old English "Readers" there's a story of a man in Topsy-Turvy Land. He walked around in Topsy-Turvy Land and found people digging down into the earth to harvest their apples, because in that year the trees happened to grow down instead of up. He poured water from a kettle on the stove and it froze his fingers because heat that day happened not to be hot. He never could tell what might happen in Topsy-Turvy Land. Fire might boil water today, freeze it tomorrow. Gravity might pull upward this moment and sideways the next. And the story ended with the man in Topsy-Turvy Land becoming stark-raving mad, not knowing what to count on at all.

A major portion of the world's suffering is caused by the dependable laws that make life possible, and keep presenting life with whole new possibilities. These same dependable laws are another of the greatest signs that we are loved by God.

But there's a <u>third</u> cause for human suffering. And it stems from the beautiful truth about <u>life's relationships</u>.

In another segment of *Fantasia* the Disney animators allow the music of Beethoven's Sixth Symphony, the "Pastoral" Symphony, to transport us to an idyllic Greek countryside populated by the creatures of Greek mythology. We see them in their various relationships: mischievous fauns playing together with friendly unicorns.....a family of winged horses—Pegasuses—parents and children.....a group of centaurs half man (half horse) and a group of their female counterparts, named by the Disney artists "centaurettes", who fall in love with each other and pair off as couples, with the help of some matchmaker cupids. Soon the comical figure Bacchus arrives on the scene atop a one-horned donkey to preside over a harvest festival. But the mythical deities in the clouds—Zeus and Vulcan—spoil it with an electrical storm that send those on earth scurrying with fear—becoming loyally protective of one another. A centaurette rescues a baby unicorn.....a mother Pegasus shelters her young.....even Bacchus and his donkey look out for each other. Then, when the storm is finally over, relationships are restored and celebrated, becoming even more precious, and life goes on together.

Relationships are the cause of much suffering. The closer I come to you, the more your experiences become mine. To the extent that I don't care a bit about you, to that extent I am free from your sufferings. But to the extent that I care deeply about you, your sufferings become my own.

To stand beside a bed where someone we love more than life itself is suffering—is to experience a kind of suffering all its own. To suffer the grief of bereavement is to feel all at once the whole, heavy weight in our heart of the immensity of our love. If we didn't love, we wouldn't grieve.

Some people—for that very reason—refuse to become deeply involved with other people. They fear the risks—the sufferings that spill over into lives that are close to each other. They try to isolate themselves into selfish little chambers where the only sufferings they can feel are their own. But they, ultimately, are the most miserable people of all.

Life's real meaning is to be found in a sympathy that grows instead of contracts. It's to be found in reaching out and caring not only about the tight little circles of family and acquaintance, but even about the larger circles of humanity itself.....so that the sufferings of the whole world cannot help but touch us with a measure of concern.....and move us to do something, however small, to help.

It is in our relationships with other people that life's deepest meaning is to be found. So much of the world's suffering has to do with those relationships. And yet those same relationships, at their highest and best—even our ability to love one another—are another of the greatest signs that we are loved by God.

Now, put on your thinking cap, and try, as hard as you can, to think of any human suffering ever endured on the face of this earth that didn't come from one or more of these three things: freedom, dependable laws, relationships. I challenge you! I don't think you can. I don't think there has been a single tragedy in human history that hasn't come from some combination of these three truths—all of which are magnificent testimony to the love of God. Everything lovely and meaningful and worthwhile in life comes from these same three factors from which our sufferings and tragedies spring. To deny the possibility of suffering would be to demolish the possibility of everything beautiful and gracious in life itself.

Well, then, what if you were God? What would you do? What could you do about the sufferings and tragedies of the world?

There's a little parable about the end of time. All the people who had ever lived were assembled before the throne of God. They were a sullen lot. They all had complaints, and they began to murmur among themselves. Who does God think God is, anyway?

One of the groups were Jews who had suffered persecution. Some had died in gas chambers and concentration camps—and they grumbled, How could God know of the suffering they had been through? Another group were slaves who had been cruelly abused by other human beings. What could God know about the indignities they had suffered? There were long lines of refugees driven from their lands—homeless people, who had nowhere to lay their heads. And there were poor people, who had never on this earth been able to make ends meet. There were sick ones and sufferers of all kinds, hundreds of groups, each with a complaint against God. What could God know what human beings were forced to endure?

From each group a leader was chosen and a commission appointed to draw up the case against the Almighty himself. Instead of God judging them, they began judging God. And the verdict was that God should be sentenced to live on earth as a human being with no safeguard to protect God's divinity. And here was a bill of particulars: Let God be born a Jew. Let God be born poor. Let even the legitimacy of God's birth be suspect. Give God hard work to do and poverty that he might know the pinch. Let God be rejected by his own people. Give God for friends only those who are held in contempt. Let God be betrayed by one of his friends. Let God be indicted on false charges, tried before a prejudiced jury, convicted by a cowardly judge. Let God be abandoned by his friends and see what it is to be terribly alone. Let God be tortured, and then let him die at the hands of his enemies.

As each group announced its sentence on God, roars of approval went up from the throng. When the last had finished, the raucous noises had become almost deafening.....and then everyone turned toward the throne. And suddenly heaven was filled with shocked and penitent silence. For where there had been a throne, now could be seen a Cross.

When it seems like God has given everything he can—our personal freedom, our law-abiding universe, our precious relationships—God goes even further.....as far as God can go. God gives himself.

Those words spoken by Jesus from the Cross—"My God, my God, why have you forsaken me?" *(Mark 15:34)*—are actually the opening words of *Psalm 22*. Jesus, in his last moments on earth, was reciting a psalm of hope. The psalmist moves from expressing his pain to declaring his faith. When God seems, to the suffering soul, to be so distant—God is, in reality, more intimate than our eyes and minds may perceive. *Psalm 22* ends on a note of triumph, with the promise of new life.....even as the next words Jesus would utter were the words of Easter morning.

Consider the conclusion of *Fantasia*. The final segment of the film pairs two radically different musical compositions. The first is Modest Moussorgsky's "Night on Bald Mountain"—which the Disney artists use to depict evil as the Prince of Darkness, Chernobog, of Slavic mythology, who rises atop Bald Mountain at night to summon the demons and the dead in a devilish dance of damnation. Here is the age-old superstitious mind's only explanation for suffering and tragedy: there must be an evil deity behind it all—a satanic power that takes pleasure in our pain and despair.

But then church bells begin to ring, heralding the dawn of morning. The music dissolves into Franz Schubert's beatific "Ave Maria". Gradually the incarnation of evil becomes just a mountain again, replaced by the incarnation of faith. We see, emerging from the fog, a procession of figures carrying lights on their way to worship the God of Truth and Light. As they move through the landscape, a bridge, a river, and the trees begin to assume the images of an outdoor cathedral. The final scene slowly ascends into a glorious sky, illuminated, we might suggest, by the love of God—who asks of us nothing more than we return God's love.

So the ultimate question about tragedy and human suffering is really not Why? but Who? Who will feel my pain with me, suffer sin's consequences with me, carry life's heaviest burdens with me? Who loves me enough to share in all my suffering, sustain me through it, and finally deliver me from it, turning my sorrow into eternal joy?

God has given us the answer—not from the detachment of a throne, but from the compassion of the Cross.....that we may know and believe that our sufferings are God's sufferings, even as Christ's final triumph has been promised to you and to me.

SOME QUESTIONS TO CONSIDER

1. Would we all be better off if no one had the freedom to do anything bad?
2. Should the Sorcerer have punished Mickey more severely for what he did?
3. Were some of the dinosaurs "good" and some of them "bad"? Why or why not?
4. If you could ask God any question, what would it be?

5. In a universe of dependable laws, does prayer matter?
6. Can we ever love someone too much?

CHAPTER 4: WHEN ELEPHANTS FLY: *DUMBO*

'For it is as if a man, going on a journey, summoned his slaves and entrusted his property to them; to one he gave five talents, to another two, to another one, to each according to his ability. Then he went away. The one who had received the five talents went off at once and traded with them, and made five more talents. In the same way, the one who had the two talents made two more talents. But the one who had received the one talent went off and dug a hole in the ground and hid his master's money. After a long time the master of those slaves came and settled accounts with them. Then the one who had received the five talents came forward, bringing five more talents, saying, 'Master, you handed over to me five talents; see, I have made five more talents.' His master said to him, 'Well done, good and trustworthy slave; you have been trustworthy in a few things, I will put you in charge of many things; enter into the joy of your master.' And the one with the two talents also came forward, saying, 'Master, you handed over to me two talents; see, I have made two more talents.' His master said to him, 'Well done, good and trustworthy slave; you have been trustworthy in a few things, I will put you in charge of many things; enter into the joy of your master.' Then the one who had received the one talent also came forward, saying, 'Master, I knew that you were a harsh man, reaping where you did not sow, and gathering where you did not scatter see; so I was afraid, and I went and

hid your talent in the ground. Here you have what is yours.' But his master replied, 'You wicked and lazy slave! You knew, did you, that I reap where I did not sow, and gather where I did not scatter? Then you ought to have invested my money with the bankers, and on my return I would have received what was my own with interest. So take the talent from him, and give it to the one with the ten talents.'"

Matthew 25:14-28

The most popular character in Walt Disney's first animated feature—*Snow White and The Seven Dwarfs*—was a child-like, speechless character named Dopey. So it was that another child-like, speechless character, with a similar name, was the star of the studio's feature, *Dumbo*.

Based on an original story—some film historians suggest it first appeared on a cereal box—*Dumbo* remains one of the shortest, and least expensively produced, of the animated features. Nevertheless, it was an immediate success with critics and audiences alike. Its title character has been a Disney icon ever since.

The story is one with which we can all identify, for it tells of the triumph of an underdog, or rather, in this case, an "underelephant". The setting is a circus. The film begins with a flock of storks delivering baby animals to their respective mothers at the circus's winter headquarters in Florida.

As the opening song reminds us—there is diversity in creation, and the stork is an equal-opportunity deliverer: "You may be poor or rich, it doesn't matter which: millionaires, they get theirs, like the butcher and the baker.....so look out for Mister Stork."

Nearly all the mother animals at the circus are blessed with a gift from the stork—the bear, the kangaroo, the hippopotamus, the tiger, the giraffe. But, sadly, Mrs. Jumbo, the elephant, waits in vain for her bundle to arrive from heaven.

Then it's time for the circus to go on tour. All of the different animals, in turn, are loaded aboard the circus train—like a Noah's Ark on rails—and the entourage begins its trip north.

At about this time, a lone stork, apparently delayed for having to carry a heavier burden than the others, arrives on the scene, searching for Mrs. Jumbo. When he finds her, he presents to her his bundle—a baby elephant—whom she promptly names Jumbo Jr.

The other elephants, congregated for this event, express their admiration for this new arrival. Then, all of a sudden, the little elephant sneezes. This sneeze causes his ears to unfold, and reveals them to be enormous—much larger than the ears of any of the other elephants.

And perhaps right here is the first thing the story of *Dumbo* teaches us. None of us is born to be exactly like the rest of us. Every one of us is unique—different in appearance, in talent, in assets, in ability. The Bible itself teaches us this. In spite of what it says about how individuals ought to treat one another equally, it's not grounded in an equalitarian concept concerning our looks and capacities and talents.

One of Jesus's parables tells of a master who bestows upon his slaves various assets. Using the social idiom of his time, Jesus is saying to us that every person has been given a different measure of talents. There are five-talent people, two-talent people, one-talent people. *(Matthew 25:15)* There are those with big ears and no ears, light skin and dark, low I.Q.s and high ones, the ambitious and the apathetic. Every personality is a unique package of abilities and disabilities—no two packages quite the same.

Equality is, and ought to be, a political concept—but it is not a description of the population. Every person's vote in a democracy should be equal—but not every person is equal, as far as her talents are concerned.

A husband once said to his wife, "I just passed Howard on

the street, and he didn't even speak to me. I suppose he thinks I'm not his equal." The wife piped up: "You certainly are his equal! He's nothing but a boneheaded bum!"

When we stop to think about it, there's a kind of sanctity in the truth that people are different. It's this truth that makes each person an individual. And here's what gives life its worth and meaning. If everyone were exactly the same—with the same talents, the same interests, the same abilities—what a monotonous ordeal life would be! Our most precious experiences and relationships would be lost, because they'd no longer be unique. We'd have nothing to accept from, or contribute to, the life of anyone else.

But because we're different, each of us must confront the truth that she, in herself, is incomplete. Recognizing that, we can enjoy, and sympathize with, and appreciate other people. Other people's talents serve us. Other people's needs give meaning to our talents. Every one of us has been given some unique combination of talents, for the benefit of others as well as ourselves—just as society itself functions through a division of labors.

When he was manager of the Pittsburgh Pirates, Frank Frisch had about as much regard for hecklers as he had for umpires. One of the box-seat occupants did a lot of grandstand managing—calling out when to bunt, when to hit-and-run, when to sacrifice, and so on. When the game was over, Frisch went into the stands and asked the man for his name and business address. The fan was flattered. He gave Frisch the information, then asked why he wanted it. Frisch replied, "I'll be down at your office in the morning with my two coaches and we'll tell you how to run *your* business." [4]

Our talents are different, our appearances are different, our labors are different—and it is because of that fact that we can ultimately work together for a larger good.

So, now, returning to the story of *Dumbo*, we learn from the start that the new little pachyderm is indeed different. Unfortunately, the other elephants react to his difference—not with wonder, but with cruelty. When they see the size of his ears, they gasp in horror, sarcasm and disdain. One of them promptly suggests that he ought to be named Dumbo instead of Jumbo, and the name sticks. In protective response, the mother elephant shuts off her compartment so that she might be alone with her very different yet, by her, very beloved offspring.

The train soon arrives at its first destination. The circus tent is erected, and then it's time for the circus parade. Dumbo does his best to follow on the tail of his mother, but his oversized ears cause him to stumble and to land in a puddle of mud. Lovingly, his mother washes him clean. Then, as the two of them appear together at the side show, an obnoxious young customer makes fun of Dumbo's ears and pulls on them. In response, Dumbo's mother spanks the boy and causes a commotion. The ringmaster orders her to be locked up as a "mad elephant".

When the other elephants blame Dumbo for his mother's misfortune, a little mouse named Timothy becomes Dumbo's friend. In an attempt to make Dumbo a star, Timothy plants an idea in the sleeping ringmaster's head. The result is the debut of a spectacular new act for the circus: a pyramid of elephants balanced on a ball. And the climax of the act will be Dumbo jumping from a springboard to the top of the pyramid.

Unfortunately, as Dumbo runs toward the springboard, once again he trips over his ears and crashes into the ball that supports all the other elephants. The consequence is a circus nightmare—with elephants cascading to the ground, and the tent itself collapsing. Back on the train, the other elephants learn that Dumbo has been made a clown, and they vow that

Dumbo is never again to be considered one of them. Thus ostracized by his own species, and further humiliated by the clowns who use him callously as the brunt of their jokes—Dumbo is made to feel inferior to them all.

And here is a second thing Dumbo's story tells us. There are always those around us who try to use the differences among us to drive a wedge between us. They point to someone else's difference as a sign of inferiority, and use it to exploit him or discriminate against him or shut him out.

Some of us know what it means to feel inferior. Maybe we've been unfairly excluded from some opportunity simply because of our looks, our race, our age, our gender, our disability. We've been told in subtle—or not so subtle—manner that we don't measure up to someone else's expectation, and are therefore somehow not as worthy or adequate as others.

A minister had just finished his first sermon in a new church. He was standing at the door, greeting his parishioners, when one man stepped up and said, "That was a terribly dull sermon, Reverend." Somewhat taken aback, the minister was haunted by that comment all week long. The following Sunday, at the end of the service, the same man came by and announced, "Your sermon this morning was one of the shallowest I've ever heard." By the third Sunday, the minister had developed a case of badly shaken self-esteem. He was understandably nervous as the same man approached him. "Were you in any way helped by the sermon today?" the minister asked. "The worst yet. You didn't say a thing." Practically crushed by that comment, the minister pointed out the man to one of the deacons and asked about him. "Oh, don't pay any attention to him," replied the deacon. "He's just a poor soul who repeats whatever he hears everyone else saying."

A girl once said to one of her suitors: "Yes, I suppose I'd like to marry you, Henry. The only thing that holds me back is a modicum of common sense." Ouch! That kind of ego deflation takes place all around us—from the husband or wife who can never do anything right in the eyes of the marriage partner, to the child who is forever belittled by her parents, to the employee who is made to feel like dirt by his boss.

Furthermore, even when others don't send us the message that we are somehow inferior, we may feel it deep down within ourselves. We're driven toward depression. Our enthusiasm is thoroughly drained by a crushing, crippling mood that keeps hammering into our consciousness the idea that we're not up to all the demands and joys of being a member of the human race. Maybe somewhere in our background we've been told to strive for absolute perfection. We've become enslaved by hypersensitive consciences. We've become victims of standards beyond human power to achieve.

Now, of course, we should always be impelled to higher living by our consciences, but we can be destroyed by a conscience that insists we attain the unattainable. We're not God. We're human beings—and that means every one of us has to learn to deal with imperfection and failure. We need to accept ourselves as the fallible, imperfect persons we are. We need to turn our self-image away from the impossible, and begin to do what is possible.

In Jesus's parable of the talents, the man who bestowed various assets to his three slaves ultimately demands an accounting of what they did with their talents. The failure of the third slave had nothing to do with the fact that the one-talent slave was less endowed than the others. After all, the five-talent and two-talent slaves were praised equally for their actions. *(Matthew 25:21,23)* The failure of the one-talent slave was his failure to act. He did nothing with his potential but bury it in the ground. *(Matthew 25:18)*

This is Dumbo's temptation. Faced with rejection and humiliation and nagging feelings of inferiority, the little elephant is ready to throw in the towel. But his friend, Timothy the mouse, won't give up on him, and tries to cheer him up. When Dumbo gets the hiccups, he and Timothy consume a bucket of water, not knowing that a bottle of the clown's champagne has accidentally fallen into it. As a result, they start seeing "pink elephants"—and when they finally return to consciousness, they find themselves on a high branch in a tall tree.

When they are unable to remember how they could have gotten up there, a group of crows suggests that maybe Dumbo flew up there. The idea crashes into Timothy like a revelation. "That's it," he shouts. "Dumbo.....your ears.....they're perfect wings. The very things that held you down are going to carry you up and up and up!"

Using a little psychology, the crows give Dumbo what they call a "magic feather". Gripping the feather tightly in his trunk, Dumbo begins flapping his ears. Lo and behold, suddenly a miracle.....he is indeed flying! Timothy and Dumbo can't wait to surprise everyone at the circus with this magnificent discovery.

The circus opens that night with Dumbo dressed as a clown atop a burning facade. The clowns expect him to drop from that great height into a bucket of foamy suds. As Dumbo begins to fall, with Timothy in his cap, the "magic feather" slips out of his trunk. For a moment he is paralyzed, but Timothy cries out to him that the feather was only a gag. The ability to fly is in Dumbo himself. Just when it seems too late—as if elephant and mouse are going to crash into the gooey bucket—Dumbo spreads his ears, and shows the world that he can fly.

The audience is stunned. He becomes an instant hero—the star of the circus—and the jeers turn into cheers. The final scene pictures the little pachyderm hugging his mother—whose love for him, and faith in him, never faltered, not even for a moment.

And here's a third thing we can learn from *Dumbo.* Some of the things for which we are made to feel inferior may be the very gifts and talents with which God has blessed us to use in a way no one else has ever dreamed.

Do you remember the ancient parable about the creation of the birds? It says that God laid at the feet of each bird a pair of wings and said, "Wear these." The birds tried them on, but—like Dumbo's ears—they felt heavy, cumbersome, awkward. Why would God give them such burdens to carry? But then, in time, the wings became bearable and, with more time, the birds began to spread them in the wind. And eventually, they finally realized that these burdens were in reality blessings that offered them the gift of flight.

It may not be wings or big ears that we have been given, but if we'll take a new perspective on whatever it is that seems to hold us back, we may discover some impetus of power that moves us forward. Think of Alicia Markova, a little girl so puny and with such weak legs that her physician urged her to dance to strengthen them, and she become a great ballerina. Or think of Glenn Cunningham, burned as a boy of seven so badly that one leg was two and a half inches too short, and only at the age of thirteen could he finally straighten it out, going on to become one of the great track stars of his time.

Above everything else, whatever gifts God has given us, they have been given for us to make a spiritual contribution to the world.

If you have visited Ivy Green, the birthplace of Helen Keller in Tuscumbia, Alabama, you have seen the well and the pump where a miracle took place. William Gibson dramatized it in his moving play, *The Miracle Worker.* The child Helen has never known anything other than a bleak and confused world of darkness and silence. Her blindness and deafness have caged her like an animal. They have kept her from even the simplest of human perceptions. No one can communicate with Helen. No one can tell her what the world is really like—why glue is sticky and why a flower is fragrant.

Were it not for the love and patience of a single person, these things would have remained mysteries for Helen probably the rest of her life. But Annie Sullivan has been struggling for months to break through this barrier—to show Helen that abstract signs on her sensitive hand can be symbols for concrete objects that hand can touch.

But how? How can one person show another the connection between two things so seemingly unrelated as that? Only by returning to all the clues together—not just once, but over and over again, even though the cost is pain and anxiety, cuts and bruises.....until the miracle happens.

And it does happen.....all of a sudden.....in the twinkling of an eye. Annie Sullivan's patience and endurance and love finally pay off.

Helen has just been dragged away from the dinner table to refill a pitcher that she had angrily emptied all over Annie. Annie pulls her outside to that water pump and forces her hand to work the handle.

Helen obeys, frightened, not knowing what she is doing. She pumps until water comes, then Annie shoves the pitcher into her other hand and guides it under the spout—and the water, tumbling half into and half around the pitcher douses Helen's hand.

Annie takes over the handle to keep the water coming, and she does automatically what she has done so many times before. She spells into Helen's free palm. "Water. W-A-T-E-R. Water. It has a name..."

And then the miracle happens! Helen drops the pitcher on the slab under the spout, and it shatters into a hundred pieces. She stands transfixed, and we can see a change in her face, some light coming into it that has never been there before.

Her lips tremble. She gropes frantically for Annie's hands and finally spells back into it the word "water". At last she understands! At last life for Helen Keller has really begun![5]

Today it's difficult to think of any five-talent, or ten-talent, or hundred-talent person—with charming personality, fortunate circumstances, physical health, swollen bank account—who can inspire us in the way a Helen Keller can. She used what little life had given her to become one of the most radiant souls of her generation.

So may it be for you and me. We were born differently—which is to say, each of us is unique. There are some who will try to use our differences to shut us out and make us feel inferior. But God is ready to surprise us by using our uniqueness to make a spiritual contribution to the world.....if we are not afraid to use our talents, however limited, in love and service.

SOME QUESTIONS TO CONSIDER

1. Are you glad that no one else in the world is exactly like you?
2. If Dumbo could talk, what would be the first thing he would want to say, to whom?
3. In what ways do people try to make others feel inferior to them?
4. Do you have a special friend like Timothy the mouse?
5. Has a burden ever become a blessing in your life?
6. If you were to be in the circus, who/what would you want to be?

CHAPTER 5:

SONG THAT NEVER ENDS: *BAMBI*

O sing to the Lord a new song;
sing to the Lord, all the earth.
Sing to the Lord, bless his name;
tell of his salvation from day to day.
Declare his glory among the nations,
his marvelous works among all the peoples.
For great is the Lord, and greatly to be praised;
he is to be revered above all gods.
For all the gods of the peoples are idols,
but the Lord made the heavens.
Honor and majesty are before him,
strength and beauty are in his sanctuary.
Psalm 96:1-6

The Disney version of Felix Salten's story of *Bambi* was nearly seven years in production. *Bambi* was previewed at a theater in Pomona, California, just weeks after the attack on Pearl Harbor. The final version was released to the world on August 13, 1942. It has stood ever since—in one commentator's words—as "the century's most beloved and enduring nature film."

There are at least three themes in the story of *Bambi* that parallel the sweep of the Biblical message—from its ancient Creation narratives to its ultimate Easter promise. The Old Testament psalmist, who was close to the land and the creatures of the field, hints at these themes in his song: "O sing to the Lord a new song...the Lord made the heavens. Honor and majesty are before him; strength and beauty are in his sanctuary." *(Psalm 96:1,5,6)*

In the first place, *Bambi* suggests, in a gentle and memorable way, that everything born is beautiful. That is to say, the natural world—creation, as God intended it—has an innocence and splendor that can only be understood through reverence and appreciation.

The film story begins with the camera eye meandering through a pristine forest at the break of dawn. A gentle breeze rustles through the spring leaves on the trees, and a distant waterfall whispers in the mist. A drowsy old owl settles into the hollow of its home as the rest of the forest creatures begin to stir. It's a new day.....and a special day indeed.....for a fawn, a baby deer, has just been born.

Other animals slowly gather to celebrate this birth and, in varying degrees, accept responsibility for nurturing the fawn, whom his mother names Bambi. In particular, a young rabbit, Thumper, takes special interest in Bambi's education—encouraging him to walk, introducing him to a world of birds, butterflies, flowers, and even a newborn skunk that Bambi calls a pretty "Flower".

To help create these scenes, a pair of fawns and other animals were brought to the Disney studio, so that the artists could study their movements and personalities. The skillfulness with which the animators capture the innocence and curiosity of this newly born deer, as well as his fellow creatures and his surroundings, has never been surpassed.

So, too, does the Bible depict life's genesis and possibility as something incomparably beautiful. With the awesome story of Creation and the idyllic setting of Eden, the scriptural message is that God's purpose as Creator is good. The psalmist echoes that confidence: "Declare his glory among the nations, his marvelous works among all the peoples. For great is the Lord, and greatly to be praised." *(Psalm 96:3-4)*

Everything born is beautiful. Sometimes parents may be tempted to doubt it. The vision of a howling face encrusted with smashed peas, protesting an overflowing diaper, may not automatically provoke the judgment of "beautiful". Sometimes we need to see beyond the skin to the soul.

Country comedian Jerry Clower told about a woman he knew down in Amite County. She lived near a construction site, and workers were putting a tar roof on the building near her house. This lady had sixteen children—or "young 'uns," as Jerry would call them. One day she lost one of her children. She got to hunting him and discovered he had fallen into a fifty-gallon drum of black roofing tar at the construction site. She reached down, hauled him up, took a look at him—then shoved him back down in that drum of tar. She said, "Boy, it'd be a heck of a lot easier to have another one than to clean you up."

Well, I hope none of us could ever say that. Beneath the grime and tar of their guilt and trouble, we can see the best in our children—if only we can perceive the beauty that was there when they were born. Is there anything in the universe more beautiful or more valuable than a newborn child?

Fred Craddock tells about a friend who was a missionary in China many years ago. He was placed under house arrest. Then one day the Chinese soldiers came and told the family that they could return to America. The family was much relieved and began to celebrate. Then the soldiers said, "You can take two hundred pounds with you." Having been in China for a long time, they were in a quandry. How could they reduce their inventory? They got some scales and the four of them—husband, wife, and two children—began arguing about what was most valuable. Here is a vase we must take. What about the new typewriter? We can't leave behind these books. After much debate, negotiation, and weighing articles on the scales, they ended up with precisely two hundred pounds of keepsake articles they would take. The soldiers asked them if they were ready to leave. "Yes," they answered. Had they weighed two hundred pounds of items they wished to take with them? "Yes." Had they weighed everything? "Yes." Had they weighed the children? "No, we didn't." Were they going to leave the children? In that moment, typewriter and vase and all those other things were virtually worthless when measured against the beauty and worth of those children.

But now, let's go on to a <u>second</u> thing that the story of *Bambi* suggests to us—and that is that <u>everything beautiful is also vulnerable</u>.

The tranquility of Bambi's story bumps into a darker reality the first time the young deer visits the meadow. Up to this point for Bambi, life has been a virtual Garden of Eden—a rich tapestry of learning experiences, nature's secrets shared in safety, with abundant food and shelter. But the day comes when he and his mother make a trip to the meadow. As they draw near, Bambi, with his youthful enthusiasm, begins to charge into the clearing. But he hears an unsettling new tone in his mother's voice as she blocks his path and calls out in warning, "No, Bambi! Wait! There may be danger on the meadow."

After venturing forth herself into the unprotected clearing, she finally decides it's safe, after all, to come onto the meadow. Bambi's education continues as he discovers there are other deer in the forest—in particular, a female fawn his own age named Feline, who takes great delight in teasing him to the point of exasperation. There, too, he meets the old stag who is his father—the leader of the herd, whom everyone calls the Great Prince of the Forest.

It is this stag who suddenly senses that danger is near and sends the others running for safety as the air is split by the sounds of gunfire. Bambi is confused, and the great stag comes to escort him and his mother to a safe place of hiding. When Bambi finally stops trembling, he asks his mother what had happened. She simply says, "Man was in the forest."

The seasons change and winter comes. Food is now scarce, and Bambi and his mother must travel once again to the meadow, in search of a few blades of grass. As they begin to eat, Bambi's mother looks up in terror. "Bambi! The thicket! Run!" With his heart pounding, Bambi begins to run as fast as he can toward the edge of the forest. "Keep running," calls his mother, "Don't look back." Just as Bambi leaps into the safety of the thicket, the shot of a rifle is heard. In one of the most poignant moments in the history of animation, we know that Bambi's mother is dead.

Everything beautiful is also vulnerable. Bambi goes on to learn that lesson in many ways—as he continues to mature into an adolescent stag. He nearly loses his own life fighting wild dogs to protect Feline, who becomes his mate. Then he himself is shot by a hunter, and when he awakens in agony, he discovers that the peaceful forest that has been his home is rapidly being destroyed by a holocaust of fire. Everything beautiful is also vulnerable.

So, too, does the Bible tell that story. From the transgression of Eden to the Cross of Christ, the beautiful plans of God keep getting sabotaged. And more often than not, the reason is that "man was in the forest". The psalmist's song of beauty and reverence is interrupted by the harsh acknowledgment of human perversity: "All the gods of the peoples are idols." *(Psalm 96:5)* Human freedom keeps getting perverted by human selfishness and sin—and the victim is the comeliness in creation itself.

So environmentalists today keep warning us of the devastating effects of human irresponsibility. Sociologists keep warning us of the explosive effects of human injustice. Psychologists keep warning us of the fracturing effects of human guilt. Criminologists keep warning us of the deadly effects of human vindictiveness.

From pockets of impotence to positions of power, the ethic of self-indulgence seems to reign supreme. A contemporary cartoon depicts two convicts wearing striped suits sitting in a prison cell. One of them looks at the other and says, "The food was better here when you were Governor."

One of the books on the best-seller list for months a few years ago was a self-help manual for success. The author advised the reader to honor greed, to not be afraid of being dishonest if one could get away with it. Morality, argued the author, is an insignificant consideration when pursuing success. In short, success is wealth, not worth. Success is limosines and a luxurious lifestyle, not integrity of character or serving people's needs. Success is getting to the top of the ladder by whatever method possible, and feeling good about it.

An apocryphal story tells of a young man who applied for a job at an advertising agency. He was told, "Your resume is full of distortions, half truths, and bald-faced lies. Welcome aboard!"

There's a streak of both viciousness and vulnerability running through the conscience of every one of us. Alexander Solzhenitsyn has written: "If only it were all so simple! If only there were evil people somewhere insidiously committing evil deeds, and it were necessary only to separate them from the rest of us and destroy them. But the line dividing good and evil cuts through the heart of every human being. And who is willing to destroy a piece of his own heart?"

Furthermore, we're vulnerable—not only to other people's sins and our own—but also to our ignorance and the very fragility of our perspective. We live in a universe of cause and effect—governed by immutable laws, and impermanent conditions. Life itself is vulnerable to the onslaught of disease and disappointment—and, finally and inescapably, death. Unless we look for a larger meaning to it all, we remain forever vulnerable to our own despair.

But this brings us to the <u>third</u> and most important thing to consider: <u>everything vulnerable is also redeemable</u>.

Bambi's forest—although it has been decimated by fire—slowly begins to recover its beauty with the coming of Spring. The animals that have survived have passed through their mating seasons, and so the landscape is filled with the signs and sounds of new life. Even Feline has given birth to two baby fawns. Bambi himself stands guard proudly on a cliff high above the thicket—no longer the naive and youthful neophyte, but now the new Prince of the Forest. And as the camera pulls back, the theme song of the movie is given words for a closing refrain:

> "Love is a song that never ends.
> One simple theme repeating.
> Like the voice of a heavenly choir
> Love's sweet music goes on."

No Disney song better describes the promises of the gospel. For the things that are shaped by egotism and greed are the things that are ultimately doomed to perish. But the relationships that resonate the melodies of God's love are eternal.

"O sing to the Lord a new song; sing to the Lord, all the earth. Sing to the Lord, bless his name; tell of his salvation from day to day." *(Psalm 96:1-2)*

Christine Fodera of Louisville, Kentucky, wrote to *Reader's Digest* about an amusing experience she and her husband had. Their priest had asked her husband, Sam, to do some rewiring in the confessionals. The only way to reach the wiring was to enter the attic above the altar and crawl over the ceiling by balancing on the rafters. Concerned for her husband's safety, Christine waited in a pew.

Unknown to Christine, some other parishioners were congregating in the vestibule. They paid little attention to her, probably assuming she was praying. Worried about her husband, she looked up toward the ceiling and yelled, "Sam.....Sam—are you up there? Did you make it O.K.?"

There was quite an outburst from the vestibule when Sam's hearty voice echoed down, "Yes, Honey, I made it up here just fine!"

So, too, was there quite an outburst that first Easter morning when an empty tomb became the doorway to the fullness of God's glory. For just as Christ taught us that love is the greatest truth in life, it is God's own love that ultimately provides us a bridge between time and eternity. Even now those we've loved who have gone before us into the grace of God—beyond our sight and our hearing—are calling out to us with assurance that they are safe in God's hands forever.

A nurse on the staff of a children's hospital told of a patient who was admitted because she was suffering from cystic fibrosis. Dorothy was only ten, but she had surrendered to the disease. All the therapy in the world couldn't generate any improvement. The hospital team tried everything to change her attitude—visits from celebrities, a new stereo. They even redecorated her room. Alas, she wouldn't respond.

Then one of the nurses showed up with a twenty-nine cent plant. It was a tawdry looking little weed, half dried-up, nestled in a cracked plastic pot. When she brought it into the room, the nurse explained what a beautiful little plant it used to be—how vulnerable it had been to a lack of human caring and concern. She asked Dorothy if she would water it, to see if she could bring it around.

What followed was a miraculous reversal. As the child centered her energy on that plant—re-potting it, watering it, turning it in the sun—her own attitude and condition began to change. Life generated life. Dorothy lived until she was seventeen. She fought a valiant fight, and inspired the lives of everyone who knew her. As this nurse told the story, "Dorothy's room became a witness to her will to live. When she died, it looked like a greenhouse!"

Everything born is beautiful. Everything beautiful is also vulnerable. But everything vulnerable is also redeemable. In the gracious arms of God are the Dorothys and the Disneys, those we've loved and those we've yet to meet.....and some day even you and me. For Christ's gospel is the good news of life conquering death with a love song that never ends.

SOME QUESTIONS TO CONSIDER

1. Is there anything beautiful about a wart hog, a tarantula, a mosquito?
2. At what time in your life did you look and feel the most beautiful?
3. Where do you think you are most vulnerable today? What frightens you the most?
4. If you were Bambi's mother, what would be the most important advice you would want him to always re-

member?

5. Is there any person alive today who is altogether beyond the possibility of redemption?
6. What is your favorite song, and what does it say about life and its meaning?

CHAPTER 6: DISNEY SOUTH OF THE BORDER: *SALUDOS AMIGOS* AND *THE THREE CABALLEROS*

You then, my child, be strong in the grace that is in Christ Jesus; and what you have heard from me through many witnesses entrust to faithful people who will be able to teach others as well. Share in suffering like a good soldier of Christ Jesus. No one serving in the army gets entangled in everyday affairs; the soldier's aim is to please the enlisting officer. And in the case of an athlete, no one is crowned without competing according to the rules. It is the farmer who does the work who ought to have the first share of the crops. Think over what I say, for the Lord will give you understanding in all things.

2 Timothy 2:1-7

In the early 1940s, when Europe was a battleground, the United States began looking south of its border, and a Good Neighbor Policy was intentionally established to strengthen relationships with Latin America. Many Italians and Germans had settled in South America, and the U.S. clearly feared the spread of Fascist and Nazi sentiment in countries of the western hemisphere.

The entertainment industry, with its loss of European markets, was eager to foster this Policy. Personalities like Carmen Miranda became stars, and the infectious songs and rhythms of Latin culture became increasingly popular.

The Walt Disney studio was invited to make a goodwill tour of South America by John Hay (Jock) Whitney, director of the motion-picture division for the Coordinator of Inter-American Affairs, Nelson Rockefeller. Whitney argued that the Good Neighbor Policy would be enhanced by demonstrating the artistic side of North American culture.

The trip ultimately produced two anthology films in the Disney library—*Saludos Amigos*, released in South America late in 1942 and in the United States early in 1943—and *The Three Caballeros*, released two years later. Both were successful, north and south of the border, and continue to enchant audiences with their montage of colors, music, live-action and animation.

Let's focus on three of the animated stories created for this pair of motion pictures.

One of them—from *Saludos Amigos*—is the story of a little airplane named Pedro. Pedro's home is a small airport near Santiago, Chile, where he lives with his father—Papa Plane, a big, powerful "male" plane—and Mama Plane, a middle-sized "female" plane. We first see Pedro sucking on a fuel line attached to a gasoline pump, much as a baby might be fed from a bottle.

The drama begins on a day when Papa Plane is too ill to fly over the Andes Mountains to retrieve the mail in Mendoza, Argentina. Papa has a cold in his cylinder-head. Mama can't go, because she has high oil-pressure and wouldn't be able to stand the altitude. So it's all up to Pedro.

"Now, remember," says his mother as he prepares to leave, "Stay out of down drafts and keep your muffler on tight."

"Don't go near Aconcagua!" warns his father. We learn that this fierce mountain is the highest and most dangerous in the western hemisphere.

After a somewhat shaky takeoff, Pedro makes a successful flight across the mountains and picks up the mail satchel on his wing. Then he turns around to bring the satchel home. But a pesky condor appears and taunts Pedro into chasing him. Momentarily forgetting his mission, Pedro pursues the bird until suddenly he finds himself face to face with the dreaded mountain Aconcagua. As the narrator describes it: "Its rocky, snow-filled crags form the face of a leering monster."

Pedro is panicked as a sudden storm breaks out—with thunder, rain and lightning. He tries to gain altitude to get out of danger, but then he drops the mail. The narrator urges him to forget the mail and to save himself, but Pedro refuses to abandon his duty. He descends into the stormy abyss in search of the satchel. By some miracle, he finds it and starts to gain altitude again. But just when it seems he has succeeded, he begins to sputter as if he's out of gas. And we see him slowly drop back into the funnel of clouds.

Meanwhile, back at the Santiago airfield, Mama and Papa plane are convinced that their son has become another martyr of the mail service, another victim of the cruel Aconcagua. But just when their hope is gone, a faint sputtering is heard in the darkness. Here comes Pedro—landing bumpily upside down—home at last! His mission—seemingly against all odds—has been accomplished.

Pedro is a hero because of his courageous tenacity. When the going got tough, this brave little plane put his own safety at risk rather than abandon his duty. In the face of overwhelming odds, Pedro refused to quit.

Long ago the author of Second Timothy had a message for a young Church that was embattled from without and within. Imperial Rome was becoming increasingly hostile to this frail community of Christian hope. And, from the author's perspective, no less dangerous were some of the misconceptions, even heresies, infiltrating the Church itself. So the author of Second Timothy reminds the reader of the primacy of one's duty to Christ, the Lord of the Church. He says, "No one serving in the army gets entangled in everyday affairs; the soldier's aim is to please the enlisting officer" *(2 Timothy 2:4).*

In other words, in the first place, one's duty to the highest authority should always take precedent over every lesser distraction. It was an incisive warning to those early "Christian soldiers" living in an ancient world that was becoming increasingly intolerant of them. It was also a crucial lesson in the days of Pedro's story, when the whole world was at war.

Life's greatest victories are never won through casual flirtation and fickleness. They call for determination, persistence, courage, self-control and tenacity.

A high school basketball coach was attempting to motivate his players to persevere through an especially difficult season. In his pep talk he asked the team, "Did Michael Jordan ever quit?" The team responded in unison, "No!" The coach yelled, "What about the Wright brothers? Did they ever give up?" "No!" shouted the team. "Did Abraham Lincoln ever quit?" Again the team yelled, "No!" "Did Abner Plumbody ever quit?" There was a long silence. Finally one player mustered up the courage to ask, "Who's Abner Plumbody? We never heard of him." The coach fired back: "Of course you never heard of him! He quit!"

The names of so many people we admire today are known to us only because they refused to be distracted by discouragement and despair. A young man wrote a children's story many decades ago and sent it to a publisher. It was rejected, so he sent it to another publisher, who also rejected it. Still, he didn't give up. He persisted. The manuscript went to a third publisher, a fourth, a fifth. In all, it was rejected by twenty-three publishers. But then a twenty-fourth publisher took a chance. And Ted Geisel subsequently became one of the world's most beloved authors of children's books—writing under the name, Dr. Seuss.

During World War II there was a plane that had been hit, not just once, but nine times by enemy fire. Although it seemed impossible, the plane kept going and survived. What was even more astonishing was the fact that all of the nine hits were from shells that explode on impact. Any one of them could have taken the plane down. The crew were so perplexed that they had the bomb squad take them apart. None exploded. Inside each of the shells there was a note written secretly in Czechoslovakian which read, "This is all we can do for you now."

The good soldier serves faithfully the highest authority—even the very Lord of Life.

Let's go on to consider the story of a little Gauchito—a young cowboy—as told in *The Three Caballeros.* He lives in the country of Uraguay. One morning he sets out to hunt for condors. Eventually he spots a nest high in the Andes from which emerges a pair of wings. However, lo and behold, these wings belong—not to a bird, but to a little donkey, a one-of-a-kind flying Burrito. The little donkey proves to be a friendly creature, nuzzling and playing with the Gauchito. Nevertheless, the Gauchito is determined to capture him. He throws his bolas around the Burrito's feet. Yet the donkey easily shakes free. Then the Gauchito tries to grab the donkey, but misses and topples over the edge of the cliff. The Burrito quickly flies below him to rescue him. Finally the little Gauchito jumps onto the back of the donkey and—after a wild ride—they bond into a team.

At that point the Gauchito decides to train his unique animal for racing. He dreams of winning thousands of pesos. The day of the fiesta and the horse-race arrives. The Grand

Prize is a thousand pesos. Knowing that a flying donkey would not qualify for the race, the little Gauchito engages in an act of deception. He ties up the burrito's wings and hides them under the saddle blanket.

All the other horses and jockeys begin to laugh when they see the diminutive boy and donkey at the starting gate. Then when the race begins and the two are left standing at the gate, the spectators join in the derision. When the Gauchito finally prods the donkey into trotting along the course, it seems impossible for them to catch up. But then—out of sight from the crowd—the little Gauchito cuts loose the Burrito's wings. With incredible speed and a cloud of dust, the pair not only catches up with the others, but passes them all to win the race.

With the donkey's wings covered again, the little Gauchito presents himself to the applause of the crowd. But just as he is about to accept the prize, the Burrito spots a bird on the top of a signpost. He spreads his wings to fly up and join it, carrying the little Gauchito on the end of a rope. When the crowd sees the deception, they become infuriated. And both the Gauchito and the Burrito beat a hasty retreat as the narrator declares: "Never to be seen again."

Through his good-natured mischief, the Gauchito has learned a <u>second</u> lesson lifted up centuries ago by the author of Second Timothy: "<u>No one is crowned without competing according to the rules.</u>" *(2 Timothy 2:5)*

The day before a crucial college football Homecoming Game the star quarterback was disqualified. The coach hurried to the dean's office to ask why. The dean said, "We caught him cheating yesterday."

"I don't believe my player would cheat," the coach blustered. "What evidence do you have?"

"He sat across from a straight A student. When their exams were compared, it was found that the two were identical on the first nine questions."

"But that doesn't prove anything," said the coach. "Maybe he crammed."

"I can answer you best," said the dean, "by the manner in which they replied to the last question. The A student wrote, "I don't know." The quarterback wrote, "I don't know either."

There is a logic written into the universe that ultimately holds us accountable for our actions and decisions. Even if we're temporarily able to hide our deceptions from other people, we can never escape the scrutiny of God. Built into the balances of life are rules that, sooner or later, reward integrity and expose deceit.

Therefore, whenever we enter a contest, we need to understand and accept the conditions that guide the competition. Above all, we need to assess the relative worth of the crown. Some crowns may not be worth the price of the contest.

Bud Greenspan, the film maker who has produced award-winning movies about the history of the Olympics, told the story of Bill Havens, a champion rower. In 1924 he was perhaps the best in the country. Greenspan said that there was little doubt that Havens would win a gold medal in Paris that year. The Olympic team was just about to leave for France, when Bill Havens' wife approached the last days of her pregnancy. There were indications that the birth might be difficult. Mrs. Havens assured her husband that she would be all right, and the doctors told him to go. But in Havens' mind the Olympic crown couldn't compete with his need to be with his wife when their child was born. He stayed at home.

Many years later—during the summer of 1952—Bill Havens received a telegram from Helsinki, Finland. And this is what it said: "Dear Dad: Thanks for waiting around for me to get born. I'm coming home with the gold medal you should have won. Your loving son, Frank." Frank Havens—Bill's son—had won the gold medal in the singles' 10,000 meters canoeing event—the very same event in which his father would have competed, had he gone to Paris. [6] And you can believe, in that moment, Bill Havens' life was truly crowned!

Our third animated story concerns a penguin named Pablo who lives with a colony of fellow penguins near the South Pole. But Pablo is an unusual penguin. Unlike all the others who love the cold temperatures of the Antarctic, Pablo can never remember a time when he was warm enough. He wears a coat, a scarf, mittens, and a huge nightcap. His closest companion is a little stove named Smokey Joe, from whose company Pablo never wanders far. What Pablo longs for, more than anything else, is to spend the rest of his life on the shores of some tropical island nearer the equator.

So one day he determines that—whatever it takes—he will go north and find the island of his dreams. As the other penguins gather to bid him farewell, Pablo begins hiking across the snow. But he hasn't gone far, when his blood begins to chill. He freezes and begins rolling downhill, knocking over the other penguins like bowling pins, then crashing back into his little igloo house.

However, Pablo refuses to give up. He starts out again—this time on skis with Smokey Joe, his stove, strapped to his back like an oversized back-pack. But when he gets to the top of a hill, this extra weight throws him off balance, and Pablo slides backward until he lands upside down in an ice crevice. Still undiscouraged, he tries it again—now wrapped in hot water bottles. But when he stops to look at a map, the warmth of his attire sinks him through the snow and ice into the water below. When his friends retrieve him, they must thaw him out of a solid block of ice.

In spite of everything, Pablo still hasn't abandoned his efforts. He gets a new idea. He cuts a boat out of ice around his igloo and sets sail up the western coast of South America. This works well for most of the journey, and he sees many landmarks along the way. He even meets King Neptune at the equator. But in these warmer waters, his ice boat begins to melt. Soon all that's left is the penguin and his bathtub, which Pablo turns into a makeshift speedboat by jamming the shower pipe into the drain hole. Finally, after all of his labors, this peculiar craft takes him to the little tropical island of his dreams.

The closing scene shows Pablo reclining in a hammock, sipping a drink and perspiring profusely, enjoying the fruit of his labors. At last, he has achieved his goal.....although, ironically, he's gazing somewhat wistfully at some pictures posted on his little shack of South Pole penguins frolicking in the cooler climate that used to be his home.

The story of Pablo suggests a <u>third</u> lesson lifted up long ago by the author of Second Timothy: "It is the farmer who does the work who ought to have the first share of the crops" *(2 Timothy 2:6)*. In other words, <u>any goal worth pursuing demands a commitment in labor and sacrifice.</u> In the famous words of Winston Churchill as he sought to rally his nation during World War II, victory does not come without "blood and toil, sweat and tears". Any cause worth a priority in life carries a price tag in energy and effort.

The reward we seek may be a military victory or a personal conquest. It may be a world finally at peace, a world free from hunger and poverty, bigotry and retaliation. It may be the elevation of human dignity or the eradication of a human disease.

In his book, *The Man to See,* Evan Thomas tells about the time in 1986 when the late Mother Teresa went to visit the famous attorney Edward Bennett Williams to ask for his financial support for an AIDS hospice. Discussing it in advance with his associate, Paul Dietrich, Williams told him that he didn't want to get involved. So the two men carefully worded a polite refusal to the anticipated appeal. When Mother Teresa arrived, she peeked over the lawyer's enormous desk and made her request. Williams listened quietly, then gave his firm, rehearsed denial. Mother Teresa's response was to say, "Let us pray." The three of them bowed their heads in prayer. After the prayer Mother Teresa started all over again and made exactly the same request. And once again Williams turned her down. Then once again Mother Teresa said, "Let us pray." Williams rolled his eyes, looked at the ceiling, and realized that they would probably be praying for months if he didn't do something. "All right, all right," he said. Out came his checkbook. In the face of Mother Teresa's persistent commitment, he finally changed his mind and promised his support. [7]

There are many battle fronts that claim the resources of the human spirit. And whatever the challenge—to nation, society, neighborhood or church—that challenge presents itself personally to each human soldier. Every single effort and every individual conquest plays a part in the larger drama that determines our destiny.

One of the turning points in the Second World War was the Battle of the Bulge. Historians point out that it was really not one big battle but a multitude of smaller battles, fought out along the Allied lines. In his book, *WW II*, James Jones describes those battles like this: "No one of these little road junction stands could have had a profound effect on the German drive. But hundreds of them, impromptu little battles at nameless bridges and unknown road crossings, had an effect of slowing enormously the German impetus—particularly in the restricting terrain of the Ardennes where there were few roads and narrow valleys and no open country. These little die-hard 'one-man-stands,' alone in the snow and fog without communications, would prove enormously effective out of all proportion to their size, in slowing down the German advance in the compartmentalized Ardennes terrain." [8]

A war cannot be won without the commitment and sacrifice of many. And in the ultimate battle between good and evil, between the kingdom of God and everything that ranges against it, the victories of faith and hope and love seek incarnation in your life and mine.

We can thank an airplane named Pedro, a little gauchito, and a cold-blooded penguin for reminding us of lessons taught long ago by a New Testament apostle who—in the challenges of life—lifted up the importance of acknowledging one's duty, of playing by the rules, of laboring faithfully in search of the goal.

Best of all, we may know that in Christ God has already given us the victory that is eternal.

SOME QUESTIONS TO CONSIDER

1. What is the "Aconcagua"—the most threatening obstacle—you are currently facing in your life?
2. Does a soldier ever have a duty to disobey his commanding officer?
3. Is it possible for a person to obey every single rule, or law, in our society today?
4. How would you like the story of the Gauchito and the Burrito to end?
5. Would Pablo have been better off if he had stayed in the Antarctic?
6. What goal in your life is worth pursuing, more than anything else, right now?

CHAPTER 7:

THE INVISIBLE YOU: *MAKE MINE MUSIC*

So we do not lose heart. Even though our outer nature is wasting away, our inner nature is being renewed day by day. For this slight momentary affliction is preparing us for an eternal weight of glory beyond all measure, because we look not at what can be seen but what cannot be seen; for what can be seen is temporary, but what cannot be seen is eternal.

For we know that if the earthly tent we live in is destroyed, we have a building from God, a house not made with hands, eternal in the heavens. For in this tent we groan, longing to be clothed with our heavenly dwelling—if indeed, when we have taken it off we will not be found naked. For while we are still in this tent, we groan under our burden, because we wish not to be unclothed but to be further clothed, so that what is mortal may be swallowed up by life. He who has prepared us for this very thing is God, who has given us the Spirit as a guarantee.

2 Corinthians 4:16-5:5

Walt Disney's *Make Mine Music*, released in 1946, is one of the Studio's cinematic anthologies. Much as *Fantasia* had used animation to visualize eight selections of classical music, *Make Mine Music* is a compilation of ten separate segments featuring some of the popular musical artists of its time.

Included in the mix are several delightful stories that were subsequently released as separate short subjects. Three of them, I think, can help us understand those words written long ago by the apostle Paul to the Corinthians: "We look not at what can be seen but at what cannot be seen; for what can be seen is temporary, but what cannot be seen is eternal" *(2 Corinthians 4:18).*

Paul is talking about our larger destiny as human beings. He's declaring that the most important part of you and me is not the physical body that everyone sees—the flesh and bones that keep changing and growing older and finally returning to dust. No, the most important part of us is invisible to the naked eye: namely, our relationships, our motives, and our potential.

Consider, first of all, the story of the Martins and the Coys, told in a song sung by the Kings Men. The Martins and the Coys are hillbilly families living in shacks opposite each other on adjoining hilltops. They've been feuding with each other ever since the morning Grandpa Coy imbibed too much "mountain dew". In his inebriated state he wanders across the valley and raids the Martins' henhouse. One of the perturbed hens wakes up the Martin family just as Grandpa Coy is juggling a mound of eggs he intends to carry home. The Martins grab their rifles and aim a volley of shots at the Coy intruder and send him scurrying for home. The Coys, awakened by the shots, begin cheering for their wayward relative's return. But Grandpa Coy tumbles down the hill after being shot.

This ignites a war of bullets across the valley. The Coys and the Martins are determined to destroy each other. As the song that tells the story expresses it, "There were uncles, brothers, cousins—why, they bumped them off by dozens." And with each casualty we see a ghost ascending to the skies, where, gathered together as families on separate clouds, they observe the continuing feud on earth.

At last there's only one person left of each family. Grace Martin, a comely lass, and Henry Coy, a burly lad, are stalking each other in the woods. But when they spot each other at close range, they suddenly become smitten and fall in love. This enrages the family galleries in the clouds, who are not eager to see the feud resolved.

A marriage unites Grace and Henry, followed by a festive barn-dance. Then the couple begin their life together under one roof in the middle of the valley between their family homes. But, alas, before too long, domestic bliss has disappeared, and the raucous sounds of belligerence have returned. The King's Men tell us in song that the couple "fight worse than all the rest—they carry on the feud just like before." And this thoroughly pleases the family ghosts in the clouds who are finally united in their pleasure that the battle goes on.

Here is the <u>first</u> thing to consider. Among the most important realities of our lives are our relationships. And yet <u>the truth about our relationships is largely unseen</u>. Although the cartoon Martins and Coys are identified by the color of their hair and dungarees, change those and you wouldn't have a clue to know who belonged to one family or another. Those fierce and loyal relationships would remain invisible to the rest of the world. Yet they would still be a driving force in that unfortunate feud.

Our relationships, our bonds of influence upon one another, remain primarily unseen by those around us, except for whatever manner we choose to express them visually. Beyond what is seen, something keeps coming and going between people—creating and affecting the shape of other personalities—engaging them in one another's lives.

Consider the engagement of a parent in the life of a child. What is seen is the result of elusive influences that cannot always be seen.

Conscientious parents, of course, are always seeking help for their parenting skills. There's a story about a student of child behavior who traveled the lecture circuit with a talk entitled "Ten Commandments For Modern Parents". In the course of time he met a young woman. They fell in love and were married. After the arrival of their first child, the man changed the title of his lecture to "Ten Hints For Parents". After the second and third children were born, the topic became "Some Suggestions For Parents". After the fourth child, he quit lecturing.

Parents may try to abide by commandments, or hints, or suggestions in nurturing their children. But what parents ARE—their habits, their values, their faith—has a lasting, unconscious influence that is far more indelible than anything easily seen. And although a parent can't control the consequences of her own influence, or eradicate the presence of other influences, she can feel a measure of identity with a child's failures as well as his triumphs—because, in a way far deeper than can be seen, that child is part of her.

We can't isolate ourselves from human relationships. They're part of us, whether we want them or not. You remember the father who said to his daughter's boy friend, "Well, young man, I understand you want to become my son-in-law." "No, sir, not exactly," replied the young man. "But if I marry your daughter, I don't see how I can get out of it."

Not all of our relationships are ours by choice. But all of them are a part of us. And we can approach each of them either with hostility or with hope. We can be like the ill-fated Martins and Coys in perpetuating old vindictiveness. Or we can learn the lessons of forgiveness and love.

Another story from *Make Mine Music* is the Disney adaptation of Sergei Prokofiev's musical tale of "Peter and the Wolf". The story begins as young Peter sets out one morning with his trusty popgun to rid the neighboring countryside of a menacing wolf. His grandfather, however, immediately thwarts the plan by dragging Peter back inside their cottage and scolding him for such a dangerous scheme. But the young hunter is not discouraged. When his grandfather falls asleep, he ventures forth again. Soon he is joined by a plucky little bird named Sasha. Together they spot a shadow on the snow-covered ground ahead that might be the wolf. Instead, it turns out to be Sonia the duck, who joins the team. Then a fourth character appears. It's Ivan the cat, who begins to chase the little bird, until Peter insists upon harmony and unity among the hunting party.

Before long the four of them find themselves face to face with the enemy—a fierce and malevolent wolf. The wolf's first victim appears to be the duck Sonia, whom he chases into a hollow tree. The wolf backs out with her feathers in his teeth. Enraged by the loss of their friend, the remaining three go on the offensive. Sasha the bird begins knocking the wolf's nose like a punching bag. But, in his retreat, Sasha flies backward into a tree and falls to the ground unconscious. Just as the wolf opens his mouth to eat him, from another tree Peter and Ivan manage to slip a rope around the wolf's tail and hoist him into the air. After some grappling, all three of them end up on the same branch, with the wolf closing in on the boy and the cat.

The scene shifts to a trio of stouthearted hunters marching nearby, carrying antique weapons. Sasha, who has regained his consciousness, demands their attention to come to the rescue. When they reach the spot, they see Peter's hat and popgun lying helplessly on the ground. But just as they begin to despair, they look up to see the boy and the cat happily in control—with the wolf trussed by the rope upside down on the branch. We don't know how they did it—but somehow they did!

As the captive wolf is carried in triumph to the village, Sasha discovers that Sonia the duck is still alive. She had successfully escaped the jaws of the predator in that hollow tree. So the story ends happily for everyone.....except, of course, the wolf.

The unique aspect of Prokofiev's story is that each of the characters in the story is represented by a different musical instrument. Peter, the young boy, is represented by a string quartet, his grandfather by a bassoon, Sasha the bird by a flute, Sonia the duck by an oboe, Ivan the cat by a clarinet, the guns of the three Hunters by kettledrums, and the dreaded Wolf by the entire brass section. As originally composed, we get to know the characters and what they're thinking without even seeing them.

So it is with you and me. And here is the <u>second</u> thing to consider. Not only our relationships, but also <u>our character—which is bound up in our motives—is largely invisible</u>. Others can see what we do. But they cannot see why we do it. We may attempt to guess another person's motives. Yet we may be dead wrong. That's why we should never be too quick to judge the motives of other people. We can make some terrible mistakes if we do.

A couple were celebrating their Golden Wedding Anniversary—fifty years of married life together. After spending most of the day with relatives and friends at a big party given in their honor, they were back home again. Before retiring, they decided to have a piece of bread and a cup of tea. The wife opened a new loaf of bread and handed her husband the end piece, the heel. All of a sudden he exploded: "For fifty years, you've been dumping the heel of the bread on me. I'm not going to take it any more.....this lack of concern for me and what I like." The wife was absolutely astounded by her husband's tirade about receiving the heel of the bread. When he had finished, she said to him quietly: "But I didn't realize. You see, that's my favorite piece."

How easily we can misjudge a person's motives. Our motives are the most intimate and complex factors in our lives. They are "us" far more surely than all the things other people see. They are the reasons why we do what we do. We sometimes do the right thing for the wrong reasons, and vice versa. It's a strange mixture of motives that operate in each of our lives.

In his later years, Thomas Jefferson was talking with a friend about signing the Declaration of Independence. When Congress was discussing independence, according to Jefferson, meetings were held near a livery-stable, and the meeting hall was besieged by flies. The delegates wore short breeches and silk stockings. While they talked, they were also busily lashing the flies from their legs with their handkerchiefs. The flies were so vexatious, Jefferson said, that the delegates finally decided to sign the Declaration at once and get away from the place as quickly as possible. The friends reported that Jefferson smiled as he told the story, because he was amused that the noblest motives undergirding that momentous event were entwined with such a practical motive as escaping the flies. [9]

So it is in the lives of all of us. Great motives combine with mundane motives. High motives compete with low motives. Some years ago a train came to a sudden stop. People started to look out of the window and then, hurriedly dropped back into their seats as they saw that the cause of the stop was a hold-up. The robbers came through the train ruthlessly stripping the money, jewelry and valuables from the passengers. One man seemed to become more and more nervous as the bandits approached the seat where he sat with his friend. Finally he took a fifty-dollar bill from his pocket, leaned toward his friend, and said, "Say, George, I just remembered. Here's the fifty dollars I owe you."

Lofty motives, selfish motives, compassionate motives, vengeful motives, motives that are holy or profane—however invisible they may be, they are part of our character. There's a stone in a village cemetery in England with this simple inscription: "To Thomas Cobb, who mended shoes in this village for 40 years to the glory of God." Perhaps no finer epitaph could be written on any of our lives than that, declaring that—whoever we are, wherever we went, whatever we did—the light of a higher kingdom shone upon our motives. Other people see what we do. Why we do it remains unseen.

The final story in *Make Mine Music* is the story of Willie the Whale, as told and sung by Nelson Eddy. It seems that a mysterious singing voice—of professional operatic quality—has been heard in the mid-Atlantic by seafaring travelers. Finally it is determined that the voice is coming from a whale, and newspaper headlines declare: "WHALE SINGS!"

The impresario Tetti Tatti is certain he knows the reason for this phenomenon. Surely the whale has swallowed a great opera singer. He—Tetti Tatti—will find that whale and rescue this captive talent. A newspaper reporting Tetti Tatti's mission drifts out to sea, where it is spotted by a seagull named Whitey, who is a friend of Willie the Whale. As it turns out, it is Willie himself who can sing. With the news from Whitey that Tetti Tatti is looking for him, Willie imagines that the impresario intends to make him a great star of the opera. So he goes to confront Tetti Tatti's ship, and auditions with an extract from *Figaro.*

Tetti Tatti—still assuming there is a human singer in Willie's stomach—orders the sailors to harpoon the whale. But they are too enraptured by the magnificent display of talent to comply with the impresario's orders. And as Willie continues to sing, we're treated to a host of delightful images of the whale's potential. We picture the possibilities. We imagine him assuming various roles at the Metropolitan Opera House: as Pagliacci in a clown's costume towering over his audience, as an enormous Tristan in duet with Isolde, as a firebreathing Mephistopheles. Given the opportunity, there are few pinnacles of performance that this virtuoso whale could not achieve.

Then, suddenly and jarringly, our glimpses of Willie's potential are shattered as Tetti Tatti—who cannot see them—manages to fire the fatal harpoon that ends Willie's life on earth.

But the narrator goes on to tell us that Willie's singing was a miracle—and that miracles never really die. "Somewhere," he says, "in whatever heaven is reserved for creatures of the deep, Willie is still singing in a hundred voices—each more golden than before." And, in confirmation of this, we hear the voice of Willie once again—this time in a heavenly setting, where his gift has come into the fullness of its potential and its glory.

There is a <u>third</u> part of each of us that is invisible—and that is <u>our potential</u>. What we may yet become is even more important than what we have become.

Jesus was able to perceive this unseen truth about people. He looked at a woman with a tarnished reputation and said, "Your sins are forgiven," and helped her move into a new life. He looked at a wobbly fisherman named Simon and said, "You are Peter, a rock," and helped him develop a character of strength and conviction. He looked at a ruthless persecutor of Christians and said, "You are Paul, my apostle," and helped him become the greatest missionary of the early Church.

Robert Ripley had a *Believe It or Note* cartoon that pictured a plain bar of iron worth $5. This same bar of iron—when made into horseshoes—would be worth $10.50. If made into needles, it would be worth $3,285. And if turned into balance springs for wristwatches, its worth would become $250,000. Believe it or not—the possibilities in just a plain old bar of iron!

The same thing is true of human personality. Because it harbors the image of God, it has infinite worth and invisible potential beyond the imagination.

Gutzon Borglum was the sculptor who planned and began the mammoth Mount Rushmore Memorial in South Dakota. One of his other great works is the head of Abraham Lincoln in the rotunda of the Capitol at Washington. He cut it in his studio from a large 6-ton block of marble. One day, when the face of Lincoln was just becoming recognizable out of the stone, a cleaning woman, who had become annoyed because she was always having to sweep around the marble, looked up at the half-done face of Lincoln. Her eyes registered wonder and astonishment. She stared at the piece, then exclaimed aloud: "How did Mr. Borglum know that Abraham Lincoln was in that rock?" [10]

Invisible within us are wonderful possibilities. And they are linked to our motives as well as our relationships. We're continually choosing between decisions that either fulfill, or are at cross purposes with, the possibilities for which God created us. As we seek to embrace those values of faith and hope and love that are the raw materials of eternity, God himself helps to carve the potential in our lives.

There's an old legend of a prince who had a crooked back. It was the source of considerable mental anguish for him. One day he said to his most skillful sculptor, "Make a statue of me, but with a straight back. I want to see myself as I might have been." When the statue was finished, it was suggested that it be set up before the palace gate, but the prince said: "No, place it in a secret nook in the palace garden where only I shall see it.

The matter was soon forgotten, but every day the prince would steal away and look long and earnestly at the statue, and each time something seemed to set his blood tingling and his heart throbbing. Months passed, and people began to say: "The prince's back is not as crooked as it was," or "The prince seems much more noble-looking than he used to be." Hearing this, the prince went again into the garden and stood before the statue. Behold, his back had become as straight as the statue's and his brow as noble. He had become the man of the statue.

Jesus Christ holds before us a vision of our possibilities in the posture of his own life. It is in the values he embodies that our true potential is revealed. Greater than any prince with a straight back and a noble brow—each of us has within us the glorious possibilities that God gives to his children. And that gift of potential is greater even than the fickleness of this earth. For in his fulfilling love, we are at home forever.

"We look not at what can be seen but at what cannot be seen; for what can be seen is temporary, but what cannot be seen is eternal" *(2 Corinthians 4:18).*

SOME QUESTIONS TO CONSIDER

1. What are the three most important relationships in your life that help to define you?
2. What long-standing feuds, like the Martins and the Coys, exist in the world today, and what hope is there of ending them?
3. Is it better to do the right thing for the wrong motive, or

the wrong thing for the right motive?

4. How do you think Peter's grandfather reacted to the news that Peter had captured the wolf?
5. If you could become more like anyone living on earth today, who would it be?
6. If you could hear Willie the Whale perform in one opera or musical show, what would it be?

CHAPTER 8:

PERSONAL PRISONS: *FUN AND FANCY FREE*

The spirit of the Lord God is upon me, because the Lord has anointed me; he has sent me to bring good news to the oppressed, to bind up the brokenhearted, to proclaim liberty to the captives, and release to the prisoners; to proclaim the year of the Lord's favor, and the day of vengeance of our God; to comfort all who mourn; to provide for those who mourn in Zion—to give them a garland instead of ashes, the oil of gladness instead of mourning, the mantle of praise instead of a faint spirit. They will be called oaks of righteousness, the planting of the Lord, to display his glory. They shall build up the ancient ruins, they shall raise up the former devastations; they shall repair the ruined cities, the devastations of many generations.

Isaiah 61:1-4

Originally released in 1947, Walt Disney's *Fun & Fancy Free* tells a pair of stories, loosely tied together by songs and commentary by Jiminy Cricket and Edgar Bergan. The first tale is based upon an original story by Sinclair Lewis about a circus bear named Bongo. The second is an adaptation of the "Jack And The Beanstalk" fable featuring Mickey Mouse and his friends in the starring roles.

Dinah Shore narrates the story of Bongo the bear. We

first meet Bongo as he is performing his circus act. He is the star attraction, and his talents are abundant. He rides a unicycle on a tightrope, juggling a host of objects while balancing on his head. He even dives from a high platform into a wet sponge.

Just as we're admiring Bongo's popularity and seemingly glamorous lifestyle, we go behind the scenes to discover that he is really—as Dinah Shore puts it—"a bear in a gilded cage". He is bound in a neck collar, "tossed around like an old shoe," and held captive behind bars. In spite of his celebrity, he is a prisoner. Locked in his cell, Bongo dreams of freedom, of being far away from the circus—able to roam the countryside and follow "the call of the wild".

Long ago an Old Testament prophet named Isaiah made a startling announcement: "The spirit of the Lord is upon me, because the Lord has anointed me; he has sent me to bring news to the oppressed, to bind up the brokenhearted, to proclaim liberty to the captives, and release to the prisoners." *(Isaiah 61:1)*

The promise of liberty and release is precious news to a prisoner. There is something about living in captivity against which the whole creation seems to naturally stand in resistance.

A man once caught a young mocking-bird and put it in a cage to hear its music. He was especially pleased when the bird's mother flew over to it with some food in her bill. Surely she would know how to feed it better than he. But the next day he was distressed to discover that the bird had perished. When he recounted the incident to a friend of his who was an ornithologist, he was told that a mother mocking-bird—if she finds her young in a cage—will often take it poison berries. It's as if she thinks it better for one she loves to die than to live in captivity.

The prison experience can be a kind of death in itself, from which the captive yearns to be free. The prophet Isaiah lived in an oppressive time when righteous individuals were unjustly incarcerated and innocent people enslaved. In Biblical days, the experience of being imprisoned was not uncommon. In fact, a significant portion of the New Testament was written in jail—including some of the apostle Paul's letters and the Book of Revelation.

Furthermore, Isaiah's promise of liberty and release is surely not limited to stone walls or iron bars or steel cages. There are other kinds of prisons—both social and personal—that hold people captive. Bongo was to discover that.

One night as the circus train is passing through some rural territory Bongo is able to shake open the door of his cage and make his escape. At last he is free! Still dressed in his circus costume, and riding his unicycle, he explores the countryside with innocent curiosity. It's not long before he discovers that the wilderness is not altogether the paradise he thought it would be. The eerie sounds of nighttime, the fury of a thunderstorm, the elusiveness of the next meal—all of them test his patience and his will to remain free.

But then he encounters a cute little female bear, Lulubelle. He is smitten at once, and she returns his affection. Before long a big, brute, burly bear named Lumpjaw appears on the scene to challenge Bongo for Lulubelle's attention. Lulubelle promptly gives Bongo a resounding slap on his face. Bongo's feelings are crushed. He has no idea—as the narrator informs us—that a slap is a declaration of love in "wild bear language". Just as she winds up to slap Bongo again, Lumpjaw gets in the way and accidentally receives her blow. The big bear immediately assumes she has fallen for him, and he is swept off his feet. Bongo quietly slips away, downhearted because of his mistaken interpretation of these events.

And Bongo's experience illustrates <u>one</u> of the personal prisons in which we may be trapped: that is, we may be a prisoner of our own mind.

John Milton wrote, "The mind is its own place, and in itself can make a heaven of hell, or a hell of heaven." One of the darkest prisons is a mind that is locked by old presumptions and false conceptions. Through no fault of his own, Bongo perceives Lulubelle's sign of affection as a sign of rejection instead. She offers him the key to her heart, and he interprets it as slamming the door shut.

We're all prisoners of the limitations of our minds. What we fail to understand holds us captive in the jail of our misunderstandings. Many years ago a group of missionaries determined they would visit a primitive tribe of people in a remote part of the world. Their goal was to teach these people more effective agricultural techniques. They could raise more food, have better nourishment, and thereby be healthier and have a better quality of life. But the missionaries were uncertain as to how they might be received. So they decided to give the tribes a gift as a sign of their friendship. They parachuted a shiny, new plow into the village as a first step to improve their farming. Then a few days later they made their way to the tribal village. What they discovered came as quite a shock. Not knowing what this strange implement really was, the tribe had erected a pedestal beneath it and were spending several hours every day worshipping it! Instead of being liberated by a productive implement, they had become enslaved to an unproductive ornament.

One of the most liberating forces in the world has always been education. There's forever something new to learn. None of us has such a command of the facts that we dare not keep our minds open. Truth is always larger than the particular handles by which we choose to carry it. A closed mind is a terrible prison.

Human history has been an unfolding drama of minds

imprisoned by old presumptions doing battle with liberating new ideas. The presumption of a flat earth with a canopied heaven was too small a prison to contain the idea of a spherical planet in a vast solar system of an infinite universe. The presumption of a feudal society governed by force was too confining a prison to incarcerate the spirit of democracy. The presumptions of bloodletting and incantations were too dark a prison to allow the light of modern medicine to shine.

The lessons history teaches us about the tragic consequences of minds closed to the liberating power of fresh truth ought to warn each of us personally against glib preconceptions and rigid judgments.

When Senator Daniel Inouye of Hawaii first took the oath of office a number of years ago, a picture of the ceremony was published in several newspapers. One of them received a critical and sarcastic letter to the editor. The writer complained that the Senator had raised his left hand instead of his right when asked to swear allegiance to his office and his country. How could such a man be trusted to serve as a Senator of the United States of America? But there was a truth neither the photograph depicted nor the writer understood. When Pearl Harbor was attacked on December 7, 1941, young Dan Inouye immediately enlisted in the U.S. Army. He fought in Italy and won the Distinguished Service Cross, the Bronze Star and the Purple Heart with clusters. When he took the oath of office as a United States Senator, he raised his left hand because he had lost his right arm in the service of his country.

Our mind—because it fails to comprehend all the facts—can make us a prisoner. So here was poor Bongo—smitten by the lovely Lulubelle—yet interpreting her slap of affection as a blow of rejection. Fortunately, the story doesn't end there. Just before it's almost too late, with the villainous bear Lumpjaw claiming Lulubelle for himself, Bongo learns the truth: Wild bears declare their love for one another with a slap. It's a love tap, not a rebuff.

With this new insight, Bongo rushes back to Lulubelle intending to reciprocate her slap. But Lumpjaw is not pleased to see this rival. He immediately tries to eliminate Bongo, but Bongo's agility and circus skills ultimately prevail over the larger bear's brute strength. Bongo, finally understanding its significance, gives Lulubelle a slap. And, we can presume, they live happily (and slappily) ever after.

The second story in *Fun and Fancy Free* begins in Happy Valley, aptly named because all the citizens are inspired by the beautiful music that comes from a Singing Harp. From the balcony of a hilltop castle, her joyous songs can be heard throughout the land. But one day a mysterious shadow falls upon the valley, and the singing Harp disappears. The consequence is that drought and depression cast a pall over the land.

We now visit the little farm of Mickey Mouse, Donald Duck, and Goofy. The trio are on the verge of starvation. Between them they have but one slice of bread and one bean left to eat. Mickey bravely cuts the bread paper thin and slices the bean into three pieces. But when Donald considers this pitiful meal, he goes berserk. He tries to eat the silverware and the plate, while the other two attempt to hold him down. Just when they think they have Donald under control, he grabs an ax and marches outside, intending to butcher the pet cow.

Donald's behavior reminds us of a second prison in which we can be trapped: we may be the prisoners of our own body.

Because we are physical beings, we are constantly under the pressure of our physical needs. The longer we go without food, the more desperate our hunger becomes. The longer we go without water, the more insatiable is our thirst. We're forever bumping up against the appetites and cravings of our body.

Indeed, there's a sense in which we can become the prisoner of our body. Our body can be our master instead of our servant. The drug addict knows the agonizing meaning of imprisonment within a body. Many of us are prisoners of various other kinds of addictions, including that common transgression of consuming more food than we really need.

A rather rotund minister decided one day it was time to shed some excess weight. He took his new diet seriously. He even changed his driving route to avoid his favorite bakery. One morning, however, he arrived at his office carrying a delicious coffee-cake. His staff all started to chide him, but his smile remained beatific. "This is a very special coffee-cake," he explained. "I accidentally drove by the bakery this morning. There in the window were a host of pastries, including this coffee-cake. I felt this was no accident, so I prayed, 'Lord, if you want me to have that wonderful coffee-cake, let there be a parking place directly in front of the bakery.' And sure enough, the twelfth time around the block, there it was!"

Raynald III was a corpulent fourteenth-century duke in what is presently the country of Belgium. He was captured in a revolt by his younger brother, and he was imprisoned. A room was built around him. It had no bars or locks. There were windows and a door that was slightly smaller than normal. Nevertheless, because of his size, the duke was unable to squeeze through the door to his freedom. His brother offered to restore his title and his wealth as soon as he was able to leave the room. All he needed to do was to lose sufficient weight to make that possible. But his brother knew his weakness. Every day he sent to Raynald's room an enormous variety of tempting foods. Instead of getting thinner, Raynald grew larger. He was a prisoner not of locks or bars or iron gates. Ultimately he was a prisoner of his own body and its appetites.

On the other hand, we may become prisoners of our bodies through vanity. Many people live in a kind of captivity dominated by beauty parlor appointments and expensive wardrobes and cosmetic devotion to their own appearance. There's nothing wrong with wanting to look our best. But there is something wrong if life's central pursuit is the coddling of our own countenance. If physical attractiveness, or even physical health, were the sole purpose of life, that battle was doomed from the start.

Yes, we want to take care of our bodies, practice sound hygiene, develop physical potential, guard against disease. Jesus himself spent part of his ministry healing bodies.....but always to teach a lesson about the kingdom of God. The most important thing—he said—is a person's faith, trust, attitude, orientation. The freedom of eternal life comes from learning to live with our body instead of living for our body. We can learn a beautiful lesson in liberation by contemplating spirits like Robert Louis Stevenson and Helen Keller and Mary Verghese.

Mary Verghese was a young surgeon in India. A terrible automobile accident paralyzed her body, except for her arms and her head. For anyone that would be a tragedy. For a surgeon it was unthinkable. But for Mary Verghese, a woman of faith, it became a challenge to do something with her body she would never have otherwise contemplated. She underwent major surgery herself, in order to be able to sit upright in a wheelchair. Then she went to work in a hospital in Vellore where she could reconstruct hands and feet and faces for the victims of leprosy. What for others would have been a catastrophe became, for Mary Verghese, an opportunity. She refused to allow her body to become her prison.

But now, returning again to our story.....Mickey and Goofy are able to prevent Donald from butchering the cow. Instead, it is decided that Mickey will sell the cow. But when Mickey returns with his proceeds, they turn out to be a handful of "magic" beans. Donald is furious and knocks the beans out of Mickey's hand, so that they disappear through a knothole in the floor.

That night a full moon causes the beans to grow with fantastic speed. When the trio awakens, they find themselves atop an incredible beanstalk in a land of gigantic proportions. They barely escape a dragonfly a hundred times the normal size. They eventually discover a castle. Once inside, they encounter its occupant—a giant named Willie. It is Willie who has stolen the Singing Harp and imprisoned her in a box for his own private amusement.

When Willie discovers them, Mickey tries to trick the giant. It seems Willie has the ability to change himself into other creatures. So Mickey challenges him to turn into a tiny housefly. Mickey and the others hope that they can swat him. When Willie discovers their intention, he locks them in the box with the Harp. Mickey, however, escapes this incarceration and, through a harrowing series of maneuvers while the giant is asleep, he is able to retrieve the key. Just as the trio are making their escape with the Harp, Willie awakens and begins an angry pursuit.

Scurrying ahead of him down the beanstalk, Mickey, Donald and Goofy use a large saw to sever the bottom of the trunk. The giant tumbles, the Singing Harp is returned to her balcony, and Happy Valley becomes a realm of contentment once again.

There's a <u>third</u> kind of personal prison in which we may be trapped—and it may be the most repressive of them all: <u>we may be a prisoner of our own heart</u>.

In a sense, this was the flaw in the personality of Willie the giant. His only concern was his own happiness. He stole the Singing Harp for his private, selfish enjoyment. He was insensitive to the well-being of everyone else whose life was affected by the music.

It's a failing of which all of us are guilty, to some degree. It's so easy to draw into ourselves and lock our heart against other people. Especially when we think someone doesn't care about us and dislikes us, we tend to do things that arouse more dislike. Then distrust breeds distrust, and hearts freeze up into little prisons of the soul. It happens in our homes, in our everyday relationships. It happens between nations and within nations.

Following the Civil War, a certain General Toombs, a rebel leader from Georgia, spent the last years of his life in a small Georgia town in company with friends and neighbors trying to figure out how the South had lost, wishing the worst for the North. When the Great Chicago Fire broke out in 1871, these malcontents actually took delight in the disaster. The old general came back from the telegraph office one day and reported the news: "Forty more blocks gone, and the wind is still in our favor!"

Too many people get locked up in their hearts—rotting in the psychological dungeon of their own bitterness and hatred. If we feel discouraged and disenchanted, if we're unhappy in our personal relationships, if we're resentful against the world.....the most liberating step we can take is a personal one. We need to open the cell door of our hearts, and study the lessons of love.

When Jesus preached his first sermon at the beginning of his ministry, it was to quote the words of the prophet Isaiah: "The Spirit of the Lord is upon me, because he has anointed me to bring good news to the poor. He has sent me to proclaim release to the captives and recovery of sight to the blind, to let the oppressed go free..." *(Luke 4:18)* Then he went on to say: "Today this scripture has been fulfilled in your hearing." *(Luke 4:21)*

What Jesus taught and lived was the truth that love is the ultimate form of freedom. The smaller the circle around our heart, the more self-centered we become—then the more suffocating becomes the prison in which we live. Yet through love our life can begin reaching out in widening circles, touching other human beings in liberating ways that reveal the power of God. For God embraces you and me with a love that is both sacrificial and unconditional.

There was a wartime prison camp where life was brutal and cheap. One day all of the prisoners were made to line up against a fence as the prison warden barked out a harsh demand: "One of you has stolen my diary. This offense is punishable by death. Who did it?" There was no response. The warden continued: "Very well. My guards will begin shooting you—one by one—until the guilty person confesses." The guards raised their rifles and pointed them at the first prisoner in the line. But before they could fire, a man at the opposite end of the line stepped forward and spoke: "I'm the man you want." The other prisoners were made to watch as the guards emptied their guns into this prisoner's body. But even before they could carry him away, another guard came running up with the diary in his hand. "Look, warden," he called out, "It wasn't stolen. It had merely fallen behind your desk." Suddenly every prisoner in that camp knew that an innocent life had been given up for him.

So, too, does the Cross remind us of a life that has been given for you and me. Even now God would open whatever personal prisons hold us captive, in order to set us free.

SOME QUESTIONS TO CONSIDER

1. Is it ever appropriate to have a "closed mind"?

2. Have you ever experienced something that stung, like Lulubelle's slap, that was really a sign of affection?
3. If you could do it, how would you change your own body?
4. What do you think about vegetarianism—not eating meat?
5. Is it important to love yourself?
6. Are people with more power, like Willie the giant, likely to be more selfish?

CHAPTER 9:
THREE DECISIVE WORDS:
MELODY TIME

Love never ends. But as for prophecies, they will come to an end; as for tongues, they will cease; as for knowledge, it will come to an end. For we know only in part, and we prophesy only in part; but when the complete comes, the partial will come to an end. When I was a child, I spoke like a child, I thought like a child, I reasoned like a child; when I became an adult, I put an end to childish ways. For now we see in a mirror, dimly, but then we will see face to face. Now I know only in part; then I will know fully, even as I have been fully known. And now faith, hope, and love abide, these three; and the greatest of these is love.
1 Corinthians 13:8-13

Walt Disney's *Melody Time*, another of the studio's anthology features, is comprised of seven separate animated segments. Each segment tells a delightful story that stands on its own. Although the film was originally released in 1948, several of the stories have become perennial favorites in the Disney library. Three of them are *Johnny Appleseed, Little Toot* and *Pecos Bill.*

Johnny Appleseed is a story of faith. Although fantasized, it's based on the true character of John Chapman, an early nineteenth-century Ohio River region pioneer who spread both his religious ideas and ample quantities of apple seeds and sprouts among the settlers.

As Dennis Day tells the story, Johnny is diligently tending his small apple farm near Pittsburgh. While he harvests the fruit, he expresses his faith in a song:

> "The Lord is good to me, and so I thank the Lord
> For giving me the things I need:
> The sun and rain and apple seed.
> Yes, he's been good to me."

As he sings, he begins to become conscious of the fact that many of his neighbors are migrating west. He, too, would like to be part of this great adventure. But, alas, he thinks of himself as much too puny for the rugged life of a pioneer. All of a sudden, a buckskin-dressed character appears and identifies himself as Johnny's Angel. He tells Johnny that Johnny has everything he needs to go west. Above all, he has faith. He also has courage and a level head. When Johnny hesitates, the Angel hands him three things that will see him through: a bag of apple seeds, a Bible, and a utilitarian pot, which he can use not only for cooking, but also as a bonnet to wear on his head.

So Johnny sets out for the western frontier, alone and on foot. Eventually in a wilderness clearing he comes upon the first little spot of fertile ground that seems a likely place for an apple orchard. He sets himself to the task of preparing the ground and planting the seed. As he works, the animals of the woods watch him suspiciously. Their experience with other human beings has instilled distrust. A skunk ventures toward Johnny, and the other animals are certain this will scare him away. But, to their surprise, Johnny pets the skunk as if it were a kitten. They are amazed. He is the first pioneer to come without a knife and without a gun. From then on, all the creatures consider Johnny their friend.

Johnny's friendships expand, as he continues to plant his apple seeds. The pioneers themselves come to know him and to love him. They begin to tell stories about him and make him a legend, celebrating his courage and kindly deeds. For, as the narrator Dennis Day puts it, "John was planting more than an apple tree. He was planting his own boundless faith. And that gave folks new heart, new hope in the job they had to do."

Johnny continues his work for more than forty years, casting across the western frontier the shadow of three blessings: "love and faith and the apple tree." We see him one day, now an old man, sleeping under one of those trees in full blossom. His Angel appears again and says there's a long trip to make. As Johnny gets up to go with him, he notices that his own body remains sleeping under the tree. Suddenly realizing that means his earthly life is over, he begins to protest that there are still crops to harvest and seeds to sow. The Angel smiles and says that Johnny is needed up yonder. They've got everything else desirable, but they're a little short on apple trees. And with that assurance, Johnny jumps up and takes the lead. He can't wait to get started on this new task that awaits him in heaven.

Johnny Appleseed is a story of faith.....faith that found fertile ground to bear fruit.

That great theologian of the New Testament, the apostle Paul, focusses on faith in every one of his letters. "We are justified by faith," he declares to the Romans *(Romans 5:1)*. "The only thing that counts is faith working through love," he assures the Galatians *(Galatians 5:6)*. And to the Corinthians he writes, "Faith, hope, and love abide, these three" *(1 Corinthians 13:13)*.

But when Paul uses the word, faith, he doesn't use it in the way so many people do—as simply an end in itself. Faith is one of those sticky concepts that can attach itself to almost anything. How often we hear people say in glucose, Gothic tones, "We must have faith!" as if that statement constituted, all by itself, the hallmark of wisdom. But what does it mean? Faith in what?

A nervous traveler once sought out the captain of a cruise ship on its way to Europe by a northern route. She asked him, "What would happen if we struck an iceberg?" "Have faith, Madam," the captain replied, "the iceberg would continue on its way as if nothing had happened." And because he used the word, faith, the woman was reassured.

The problem of the world has never been to have more faith. We have all the faith we can use. The real problem is its misdirection. Faith itself is something intrinsic to our nature. It's as integral a factor in our lives as eating and sleeping and breathing. People believe, trust, put their faith in all kinds of things: ouija boards, vegetarianism, racial supremacy, reincarnation, noblesse oblige, salvation by narcotics, the "power of the almighty dollar," Weight Watchers, motherhood, vitamin C, "my country—right or wrong," fate, law, chance. There's little or nothing in which people, however sophisticated, will not put their faith.

And there are always those around who are ready to exploit this inborn human capacity for faith. How many products in the commercial marketplace advertise themselves as "something to believe in," or "something you can really trust," or "something in which celebrities put their faith"? Invariably this claim is followed by some testimonial—perhaps as dubious as that of the man who sent in this letter: "Before I used your hair tonic, I had three bald spots. Now I have only one."

No, faith is not something of which we need more. It's something we already have in abundance. What we need is an adequate and ultimate object for our faith.

When the apostle Paul uses the word, faith, he means faith in God. But here again, the word, God, can connote many things. God has been described by philosophers and theologians with phrases like "First Principle," "The Unknown Absolute," "Process of Integration," "Ground of All Being," "Fundamental Substance," "Elan Vital," "The Power not ourselves that makes for Righteousness," and so on. There's been a sense of God running through the minds and hearts and vocabularies of most thinking women and men since the beginning of time.

But few of us are willing to put our faith in a word or a phrase. So here is where Paul points us to a person and says, God is the God of Jesus Christ. This is where our faith supremely belongs—not with some semantic concept, not with our own self-sufficiency—but with the God whose grace is as profound as Christ's compassion on the Cross, and whose promise is as powerful as Christ's victory over death.

John Chapman, the real-life Johnny Appleseed, was greatly influenced by the Swedish theologian, Emanuel Swedenborg. Another famous person who studied the teachings of Swedenborg was Helen Keller. After she had learned to communicate—in spite of being deaf, dumb, and blind—she was visited by Phillips Brooks. Brooks was the dedicated Boston cleric who, among other things, wrote the carol, "O Little Town Of Bethlehem". While Annie Sullivan, Helen's faithful companion, interpreted his words, Brooks talked to Helen Keller about the life and teachings of Jesus. Soon a broad smile covered Helen's face. She wanted to respond. Through her interpreter, she said, "I knew all about God before you told me, only I didn't know his name." [11]

This, says the apostle Paul, is what faith in God means. We can trust God unreservedly, because in the life and countenance of Jesus Christ the faithfulness of God himself is revealed.

Little Toot is a story of hope. The tale is sung by the Andrew Sisters. Little Toot is a small New York Harbor tugboat. He lives with an ardent hope. He hopes to become a worthy and noble tug like his father, Big Toot, who guides the large ships in and out of port. The trouble is, there's a streak of immaturity in Little Toot. He enjoys playing little pranks, such as making traffic-stopping figure-eights in the water and blowing smoke rings around the portholes of other vessels.

But then one day he resolves to grow up and achieve his hope. He spots his father, Big Toot, performing the tugboat's duty, escorting an ocean liner out to sea. Little Toot decides to assist. He positions himself behind the enormous ship's rudder and begins to push. But he only succeeds in turning the ship entirely off course. It loses control and crashes into the city streets bordering the harbor, causing a terrible disaster.

As punishment, Little Toot is banished from the harbor. He is escorted by police boats out to sea. He passes his father, whose name is now disgraced. Big Toot has been demoted to pulling a garbage barge. When they pass beyond the twelve-mile limit, Little Toot is left alone by the police boats in choppy waters.

As he bobs dejectedly in the sea, the skies turn dark. A violent storm breaks out. He's tossed from wave to wave. Then he notices the flare of a ship's distress rocket. A huge ocean liner is in danger of crashing on the rocks. The ship sends out an SOS signal, which reaches the other tugboats in the harbor. But when they attempt to come to the rescue, huge and ferocious waves prevent their progress. The only hope is Little Toot himself.

Courageously the small tug pushes his way toward the imperiled ship. A rope is tossed from the deck. With the rope attached to himself, Little Toot struggles mightily to pull the liner to safety. It seems like a hopeless task, but Little Toot refuses to surrender hope. Just when everything seems lost, a bolt of lightning charges the tug with sufficient power to move the ship. With that inertia, Little Toot begins the long and arduous task of bringing the ship to shore.

When he finally arrives with it safely in the harbor, he is cheered as a hero. His hope has been fulfilled. He has become a faithful and reliable tugboat, just like his father, whose own reputation is now restored.

Little Toot is a story of hope.....hope that turns tragedy into triumph.

The apostle Paul also speaks of hope throughout his New Testament letters. "Put on...for a helmet the hope of salvation," he advises the Thessalonians *(1 Thessalonians 5:8)*. There is "hope laid up for you in heaven," he promises the Colossians *(Colossians 1:5)*. And, again, his words to the Corinthians are these: "Faith, hope, and love abide, these three" *(1 Corinthians 13:13)*.

Surely hope is something we desperately need in our time. Life for so many people is no more promising than the vital statistics in a newspaper—births, marriages, deaths.....or, as one local journal put them, "Hatched, Matched, and Dispatched." The front page usually tells us very little that is hopeful about human nature. People are exploiting each other, robbing each other, suing each other, slandering each other, murdering each other.

The story is told of a ship that discovered a shipwrecked sailor who had survived several years on a deserted South Sea Island. A small boat from the ship put out for the island. When it landed on the beach, the officer in charge threw the sailor a bundle of recent newspapers, and said: "Read through these and then let us know whether you still want to be rescued."

Nevertheless, we cannot escape hopelessness simply by isolating ourselves from the world. We can't sit back and pretend we have no share in society's problems nor any responsibility for the lives of people around us. There's no hope to be found in becoming self-centered and lazy. I remember asking an undertaker about his most unusual interment. He guessed it was the widow who complained that her husband had been the laziest man on earth. So she had him cremated and put him in an hour glass. There's no salvation from hopelessness through laziness or self-centeredness.

A kindhearted elderly woman kept noticing a very down-and-out sort of man standing at the corner of the street near her residence. One morning she took compassion on him, and pressed a dollar into his hand, and whispered, "Have hope!" The next time she saw him, he stopped her and slapped thirty dollars into her hand. "What does this mean?" she asked. "It means, ma'am," he said, "that 'Have Hope' came in first at thirty to one."

Hope is the vision of victory. And the kind of hope that emerges from the apostle Paul's faith in God is eternally confident. For it has the vision of Easter morning. It has the assurance that the future ultimately belongs to God. It can begin to look beyond the perils of life to its possibilities, always expectant and grateful for what lies ahead.

When Leopold Stokowski celebrated his ninetieth birthday, someone asked the great orchestra conductor if there was anything to which he looked forward. "By all means!" he declared with a smile. "The next rehearsal!"

This, says the apostle Paul, is what hope means: that we have a claim on the future, because God has a claim on each one of us. And the future belongs to God.

Pecos Bill is a story of love.....a tall tale about love, but love nonetheless.

Roy Rogers and the Sons of the Pioneers tell the folk legend of this mythical figure of the Old West. When he's only a baby, Bill is bumped out of a covered wagon beside the Pecos River in the Texas desert. No one in his family notices, and the wagon rolls on. So, at a tender age, little Bill must fend for himself. He makes his way into a cave where a mother coyote comes home to feed her young. When he sees her, Bill looks up and grins, and Ma Coyote immediately begins to love him as one of her own.

Thus raised as if he belonged to the coyote pack, Bill learns all the skills of the animal kingdom. Indeed, eventually he can outperform every one of the other creatures. As the narrators tell us: "He out-loped the antelope, out-jumped the jackrabbit, and even out-hissed the rattlesnake."

One day Bill spots a pony that is being attacked by vultures. Bill enters the fray, and saves the beleagured pony. They immediately become inseparable companions and the closest of friends. They grow up together and accomplish incredible feats. Bill ropes a cyclone, rides it and tames it down to a breeze. When a drought hits Texas, he rides to California and lassoes a large enough rain cloud to solve the problem. When he becomes thirsty in the desert, he gets a stick and digs the Rio Grande River.

Then the day comes when Pecos Bill's life is changed forever. He is introduced to the lovely and nimble Slue Foot Sue. It's love at first sight. Bill begins to court Sue, arousing jealousy in his horse—now known as Widowmaker—who resents no longer being the center of attention in Bill's life. Bill proposes marriage, and Sue accepts, with one stipulation. She wants to be wed while riding Widowmaker.

The wedding day arrives. Sue is dressed in her finest outfit, enhanced by a springy bustle. It is obvious as she approaches Widowmaker that the horse is anything but pleased.

With fire in his eyes, he's going to toss her as far as he possibly can. But Sue is a natural bronco-buster, and she gamely stays in the saddle.....until all the bouncing begins to build up in her bustle. Then, all of a sudden, she is bounced into the air. She lands on the ground bustle-first, propelling her back up into the air. Each time she bounces down and up again, it becomes apparent that she's gaining altitude. Bill tosses out his trusty lasso to stop her, but for the first time in his life, he misses. Unknown to him, we see where Widowmaker has stepped on the rope to thwart its accuracy.

Sue keeps bouncing and bouncing until finally she comes to the moon. And that's where she finally stops. This is a source of great sadness to Bill, for there's no way to bring her back. From that time on, he returns to live with the coyotes. And every night when the moon comes up, all the coyotes join Pecos Bill in howling at the moon, declaring his love for the woman he lost.

Pecos Bill is a story of love.....love that changes lives and transcends the changes of life.

The apostle Paul also has much to say about love. "Be of the same mind, having the same love," he counsels the Philippians *(Philippians 2:2)*. "I pray that you may...know the love of Christ that surpasses knowledge," he writes to the Ephesians *(Ephesians 3:18-19)*. And recall again his words to the Corinthians: "Faith, hope, and love abide, these three" *(1 Corinthians 13:13)*.

Love, however, is another of those words that gets applied to just about everything, from lust and lavender perfume to jazz and junk food. A teacher asked one of her young pupils to explain the difference between liking and loving. The child responded, "Well, I like my parents. But I love pizza!"

However sloppy we may be in our use of the word, Paul identifies love with God. But he doesn't say that love is God. He says that God is love. In other words, we can't simply compound our fuzzy, sentimental ideas about love and assume they are adequate enough to describe God. It is God who ultimately defines love. God's total and unconditional love, revealed in the life and death of Christ, puts to shame all our imperfect desires and affections.

Yet that love is God's own gift to each and every one of us. It is the sanctification of our reality as human beings. It reveals that the highest meaning of life is to be found in our relationships. It beckons us to embrace one another with affirmation, forgiveness, and commitment.

The Irish poet Thomas Moore loved his wife. She was the beautiful actress Bessie Dyke. She may have felt that her beauty played a critical role in making her attractive to her husband. The story is told that Moore had to be away from home on an overseas trip, which in those days took many months. While he was gone, Bessie contracted the dread disease of smallpox. It covered her beautiful face with scars. She was brokenhearted and afraid that her husband would be repelled by her ugliness. In fact, she was so afraid that she couldn't even write to tell him what had happened. A family friend did write to Moore and apprise him of what had happened. Moore could immediately imagine the torment in his wife's mind. He sat down and wrote a poem, which he sent to Bessie immediately. It was originally meant for her alone:

> "Believe me, if all those endearing young charms;
> Which I gaze on so fondly today,
> Were to change by tomorrow and fleet in my arms,
> Like fairy-gifts fading away,
> Thou wouldst still be adored, as this moment thou art;
> Let thy loveliness fade as it will,
> And around the dear ruin each wish of my heart
> Would entwine itself verdantly still"

So does God make that promise to you and me.

"Faith, hope, and love abide, these three; and the greatest of these is love!"

SOME QUESTIONS TO CONSIDER

1. Is it possible for a person to have too much faith?
2. If you could ask Johnny Appleseed one question, what would it be?
3. How would you complete the sentence: "Life without hope is..."?
4. Should a parent, like Big Toot, be punished for the mistakes of a child, like Little Toot?
5. Has love ever gotten you into trouble?
6. Why was Widowmaker jealous of Slue Floot Sue? Is jealousy ever justified?

CHAPTER 10:
INHERITANCES:
THE ADVENTURES OF ICHABOD AND MR. TOAD

Once when Jacob was cooking a stew, Esau came in from the field, and he was famished. Esau said to Jacob, "Let me eat some of that red stuff, for I am famished!" (Therefore he was called Edom.) Jacob said, "First sell me your birthright." Esau said, "I am about to die; of what use is a birthright to me?" Jacob said, "Swear to me first." So he swore to him, and sold his birthright to Jacob. Then Jacob gave Esau bread and lentil stew, and he ate and drank, and rose and went his way. Thus Esau despised his birthright.

Genesis 25:29-34

Now Jacob looked up and saw Esau coming, and four hundred men with him. So he divided the children among Leah and Rachel and the two maids. He put the maids with their children in front, then Leah with her children, and Rachel and Joseph last of all. He himself went on ahead of them, bowing himself to the ground seven times, until he came near his brother.

But Esau ran to meet him, and embraced him, and fell on his neck and kissed him, and they wept.

Genesis 33:1-4

Walt Disney's *The Adventures of Ichabod and Mr. Toad*

is a two-part animated feature based on a pair of literary classics: Washington Irving's "The Legend Of Sleepy Hollow" and Kenneth Grahame's "The Wind In The Willows". It was the last of the Disney "anthology" features—those films which combine two or more unrelated stories in the same motion picture.

Although second in the order of the feature, let's begin with *Ichabod.* Bing Crosby narrates the story of Ichabod Crane, the itinerant schoolteacher who arrives in the New York district known as Sleepy Hollow. Lean and lanky, he resembles a scarecrow with a snipe-like nose.

Ichabod's skinniness, however, disguises his enormous appetite for the pleasures of life. In his classroom, he favors the children whose mothers are excellent cooks. In consequence, he's invited into many a home to share delicious dinners. Ichabod also offers singing lessons to the young ladies of the community. They, too, provide him with a constant meal ticket.

Then one particular maiden in the village catches his eye. Katrina Van Tassel is not only lovely—she is the daughter of the wealthiest farmer in the region. It's this latter quality that most attracts Ichabod, as he imagines himself stepping into the family inheritance. He sets out to win the affections of this girl, who comes with such a rich prize.

But he has a rival. Brom Bones is the burly and popular "man about town". He, too, has his eyes on Katrina. There's much jockeying back and forth between the rivals—with Ichabod, through remarkable agility and slipperiness, usually coming out on top.

Then on Hallowe'en night there's a party at the Van Tassel home. There, too, Ichabod upstages his rival by demonstrating his talent on the dance floor. However, in the course of the evening, Brom Bones observes Ichabod tossing spilled salt over his shoulder. Realizing how superstitious Ichabod must be, Brom proceeds to tell the local "ghost story" with great flourish. It concerns a terrifying Headless Horseman, who rides in the hollow on this one night of the year in search of another head.

After hearing the story, a frightened Ichabod must now travel home through the hollow, alone except for his horse. As he ambles along, every owl hoot or frog croak sends shivers down his spine. A galloping sound panics him, until he discovers it's nothing more than a collection of pussywillows knocking in the wind on a hollow log. He dissolves into nervously hysterical laughter.

Then suddenly a more sinister laugh catches his ear, and he turns to see the nightmare he has been dreading. The Headless horseman is a huge black figure atop a fierce black stallion. He is carrying a sword in his right hand and a flaming pumpkin head in his left. A frantic chase ensues, with Ichabod finally crossing the bridge that is supposed to offer safety. But as he looks back, the Horseman hurls the pumpkin head toward him. The next morning nothing is found but Ichabod's hat and pieces of a pumpkin.

The story ends with Brom Bones being wed to Katrina. The narrator explains that no one really knows what happened to Ichabod. One rumor suggests that he moved to another county and married a wealthy widow. But the local townspeople insist that he was spirited away by the Headless Horseman.

There's a Biblical story that also concerns rivals for a significant inheritance. In this case, the rivals are two brothers named Esau and Jacob. The inheritance in question is the birthright of their father Isaac. This birthright has profound implications in the Old Testament, for it represents the Covenant God has established with the descendants of Abraham, as well as God's promise of the land of Canaan. As the oldest son, Esau would have a natural claim on this family birthright. But his younger brother Jacob covets this inheritance for himself.

This suggests the <u>first</u> of several truths illustrated in these stories. <u>Life is a blend of what we inherit and what we do with what we inherit</u>.

Ichabod Crane, the Sleepy Hollow schoolmaster, had inherited many talents. He could teach, and he could sing. He could impress the ladies with his charm and dancing. But he used that legacy of talent in a venal pursuit of a rich farmer's daughter and estate that were ultimately inherited by someone else.

Ichabod also inherited a superstitious nature. His life revolved around a variety of unnatural and irrational fears. Spilled salt had to be tossed over one's left shoulder to avoid a horrible fate. We can only speculate about all the other phobias Ichabod may have had. Perhaps the Headless Horseman is a symbol for them, sealing his fate.

Every one of us has inherited assets and liabilities in life. Even before the moment of our birth, we have received a physical inheritance that will accompany us as long as we live on earth. A physician was asked about the best way to prevent heart disease. "That's easy," he replied, "Have parents with healthy hearts." In matters of health, we continue to learn more and more about the importance of family history. There's an inheritance of strength and weakness written into our genetic makeup. What we do with that inheritance is no less crucial.

We sometimes deceive ourselves into thinking we are "self-made" individuals. This is a particularly gratifying perspective if we have been blessed with success. Surely if we are a giant in the corporate world, it's entirely because of our own abundant wisdom and industriousness. Surely if we are a famous movie star, it's completely due to our own gorgeous appearance and talent. Surely if we are a powerful political figure, it's totally the consequence of our own virtue and insight.

Yes, we should always endeavor to do something positive with the talents and resources that have been given to us. But that's just the point. A large measure of those talents and resources are gifts. We have inherited them from others, from friends, from family, from God. In the ultimate scheme of things, we have more debts than debtors.

A prominent entrepreneur was once asked to explain his success. He replied candidly that he had done it all through hard work, careful planning, and his inheritance of ten million dollars. Behind every breath-taking "Horatio Alger story" of success lies a subtle drama of great gifts, good fortune, and endebtedness to others.

The freedoms of our society, the glories of nature, the inspiration of the arts, the nurture and support of the institutions that shape our lives—these are largely gifts we have inherited. What we do with them—how we cherish them and perpetuate them and enhance them—that's what counts.

When he was President of Williams College, Mark Hopkins was approached by a wealthy student who had been involved in causing some property damage. The student flippantly offered to pay for the damage he had caused. Hopkins was indignant. He replied: "Rich young men come here and take that tone as if they could pay for what they get here. No student can pay for what he gets at Williams College. Who can pay for the sacrifice of Colonel Williams and all the other benefactors? Every one here is a charity student!"

So are we all ultimately charity cases in life—inheritors of abundant gifts for which we should be profoundly grateful. What we do with that inheritance is decisive in our destiny.

With that in mind, let's go on to the story of *Mr. Toad*, as told by Basil Rathbone. We first meet Toad's friends Rat and Mole as they sit down in Rat's riverfront home to share afternoon tea. A knock on the door interrupts the scene. It is a special delivery message from Angus MacBadger summoning them to Toad Hall.

Toad Hall is the inheritance of J. Thaddeus Toad. This ancestral home is a stately mansion, considered to be the finest in the district. All of the animals are extremely proud of it. But it is in jeopardy. Toad has come to the brink of bankruptcy. The problem is that Toad himself is a reckless and impulsive personality, following every fad without counting the cost. In an effort to save Toad Hall, MacBadger has volunteered to try to settle Toad's accounts.

When Rat and Mole arrive, MacBadger explains the latest crisis. Toad has a new mania. He is rampaging around the countryside in a gypsy cart with a horse named Cyril. We see the two of them—Toad and the horse—happily and irresponsibly travelling at full gallop, knocking down fences, hedges, a clothesline and a greenhouse along the way. They come to a halt when they spot Rat and Mole standing beside the road in front of them. Toad introduces these two old friends to his new equine friend, named Cyril Proudbottom, and invites them to hop aboard and go for a ride. Declining the invitation, Rat gives Toad a lecture on the foolishness of his new fad. Toad ignores it and continues on his way.

Suddenly an unusual sound catches Toad's attention. Coming down the road is a motor-car, the first that Toad has ever seen. His eyes begin to spin. He must have one for himself. Rat and Mole find him sputtering on the ground in imitation of a rattling jalopy—his newest obsession. They proceed to escort him back to Toad Hall and lock him in his room, hoping that this latest mania will work its way out of his system.

However, Toad escapes out the window. We next see newspaper headlines declaring that Toad has been arrested for stealing a car. A courtroom trial is convened. The Counsel for the Crown calls Rat and Mole as witnesses. He forces them to reluctantly testify that they had locked Toad up to prevent him from acquiring a car. He also calls MacBadger, who can't get a word in edgewise. But the Prosecutor makes it clear that, since MacBadger had cut off Toad's allowance, Toad could not have had any money to buy a car. With that, the prosecution rests.

Toad then rises to act as his own counsel and present his own defense. His first witness is Cyril the horse, who proceeds to tell us what really happened. After Toad escaped from his locked room, he and Cyril were walking along the road together when they were passed by a bright red motor-car containing a bunch of weasels. The car stopped at a bar run by a certain Mr. Winkie. Toad and Cyril followed the weasels into the bar. Not knowing the car had been stolen, Toad tried to buy it. However, he had no cash. So he proposed a trade, which the weasels gladly accepted and Mr. Winkie witnessed: a trade of the car for the only thing Toad had to offer, Toad Hall, his inheritance.

The courtroom is aghast. MacBadger faints. The Prosecutor mocks Toad. Does Toad expect anyone to believe that he traded a landmark estate worth a hundred thousand pounds for a mere motor-car? Would someone give up such a valuable inheritance for the mere whim of the moment?

Well, according to the Old Testament book of Genesis, someone would indeed do just such a thing! Here we go back to the story of Esau and Jacob, the sons of the patriarch, Isaac. As the oldest son, Esau had the claim on the family birthright—this special inheritance in property and name.

But, according to the story, one day Esau came in from the field feeling famished. His younger brother Jacob happened to be cooking some stew at the moment, which must have smelled delicious. Esau asked for a helping. Jacob, however, was very shrewd. He saw that he could take advantage of his brother's hunger and impulsiveness. So he suggested a trade: Esau's birthright for some of the stew. And, obsessed as he was at that moment, Esau agreed. He forfeited this most magnificent of inheritances—this sacred birthright—for a bowl of stew!

And here's a <u>second</u> truth—and very incisive warning—in the stories of both Mr. Toad and Esau: <u>Impulsive decisions can be foolish decisions!</u> Unless we're careful, we may find ourselves sacrificing an ultimate inheritance because of an immediate obsession.

A little boy had been given a gift of money by his grandmother. It was exactly enough to purchase the new bicycle he wanted, when it went on sale the following month. He counted the cash every day, and every evening he knelt beside his bed and offered this prayer: "Lord, thank you for this gift from Grandma, and please, Lord, don't let the ice cream man come down our street tomorrow."

Great plans and ultimate inheritances can sometimes be sabotaged by the appearance of the ice cream man and the temptation of an immediate obsession.

Many people today share Mr. Toad's fixation on speed and the latest, fastest mode of transportation. They're forever in a rush. They see life as a race with destiny. So they try to cram into it as much as possible. They want the fastest computer, the fastest diet, the fastest service, the fastest education, the fastest headache relief. And they want it now! Yet, as Mahatma Gandhi reminded us, "There is more to life than increasing its speed." An obsessive concern for velocity can interfere with a commitment to veracity.

A young Ensign was given the opportunity to demonstrate his ability to get a destroyer on its way. He issued his commands and sent the sailors scurrying in all directions. In record time, the ship was steaming out the channel on its way to its destination. Soon a seaman approached him with a message from the captain. He was surprised, however, that it was a radio message. It read: "My personal congratulations upon completing your underway preparation exercise with amazing speed. In your haste, however, you have overlooked one of the unwritten rules: make sure the captain is aboard before getting under way."

Our immediate obsession may cause us to forfeit our most valuable possession. A star athlete is arrested for drug trafficking. Ultimately he had it made—but he blew it for something immediate. A successful business executive embezzles a sum of money. Ultimately she had it made—but she blew it for something immediate. A popular politician commits a carnal indiscretion. Ultimately he had it made—but he blew it for something immediate. How foolish and tragic it can be when our preoccupation of the moment causes us to sacrifice an inheritance far more ultimate.

So, in the trial of Mr. Toad, there is anguish and disbelief throughout the courtroom over Toad's foolishness in his impulsive decision to exchange his entire estate for a motorcar. Nevertheless, such foolishness—at least in this case—is not illegal. So Toad calls his second witness, Mr. Winkie, to corroborate the truth of what happened.

Yet, shockingly, Winkie perjures himself and tells the court that it was Toad who tried to sell HIM the stolen motorcar. Pandemonium breaks out. Toad is declared guilty and given a long prison term in the Tower of London.

Time passes. Christmas comes and finds Toad languishing in the Tower. He resolves to henceforth curb his obsessions and become more responsible. Then Cyril shows up with a disguise that allows him to escape. The chase is on, with the police in hot pursuit. Toad steals a train, tosses himself off the train into the river and finally makes it to Rat's home, where his friends have been thinking about him. Rat advises Toad that he should probably give himself up.

Then, all of a sudden, MacBadger appears with the news that the weasels have taken over Toad Hall. And Winkie is their leader! Because the car had indeed been stolen by them, rather than by Toad—the trade had to be illegal. Toad Hall might yet be saved. Then follows an action-filled sequence at Toad Hall pitting the quartet of Rat, Mole, MacBadger and Toad against Winkie and the weasels. The prize is the deed of trade, which proves Toad's legal innocence. Through much mayhem and mishap, our foursome finally retrieve it. Toad Hall is saved, justice is served, friendships are celebrated, and Toad himself has promised to reform.

Nevertheless, our last glimpse of Toad is aboard a turn-of-the-century biplane. With Cyril at his side, he is flying across the countryside, knocking over chimneys and statues and anything else in his way. He has survived, only to pursue a new mania. And his friends can only shake their heads, imagining what new crisis may lie ahead. But as before, we know they will stand by him to the end.

And here's a third and final observation to be made. The greatest inheritance we can receive or bestow is the gift of friendship and forgiveness. Rat and Mole and MacBadger had stood by Toad in spite of, and without approving of, his foolishness. They had worked together as a team to clear his name and save Toad Hall. And even though Toad's promise to reform seemed short-lived, we can be sure that his friends will not be far away.

One of the great passages in the Bible is the account of Esau's reconciliation with Jacob. Decades have passed since Jacob weaseled the family birthright away from Esau with the stew. Because of that incident and another unscrupulous act of deception against his brother, Jacob has been living away from Palestine for the last twenty years. When he decides to return, he does everything he can to protect himself and appease his brother. But to his surprise and enormous relief, Esau greets him with forgiveness. In the words of Genesis: "Esau ran to meet him, and embraced him, and fell on his neck and kissed him, and they wept." *(Genesis 33:4)*

No close relationship—friends, brothers, sisters, family—can survive for long without the presence of forgiveness. None of us is infallible. We all need to be forgiven for things we have done or failed to have done. Likewise, those with whom we share loving relationships need our forgiveness as well.

That's not to say that forgiveness is always easy. Anyone who considers forgiveness to be easy is dangerously close to sanctioning whatever he says he is forgiving. Much that passes for forgiveness in the moral realm is, in reality, simply tolerance and acceptance of immorality. It's easy to forgive something we don't take very seriously ourselves. But it's difficult to forgive that which does damage to what we cherish.

Here's the dilemma of a parent raising a child. Much as she loves her child, and wants to forgive his every transgression, she would be an irresponsible parent if she always said, "Never mind, it doesn't matter." It would be as if to say, "I don't care what you do. I don't care what kind of person you become. You're not that important to me." Easy forgiveness is not to be confused with love. Discipline and denial are signs that love sometimes needs to be "tough".

Nevertheless, difficult as it may be, parents who love their children are ultimately ready and willing to forgive them. The poignancy of such forgiveness has the power to communicate a profound lesson about the depth of their love. And it is the greatest inheritance a child can receive.

Years ago a rebellious young man committed a serious crime. His parents spent all their savings and more in attorney fees. But the boy was sent to prison. His father and mother went to visit him in jail, but the boy refused to see them. They wrote to him daily, but the letters were returned unopened. The day finally came when the young man was released. He boarded a train going west, hoping to start a new life. While on the train, he began thinking about his parents. He was suddenly flooded with remorse. He knew how terribly wrong he had been.

The train was going to pass through his old home town. He desperately wanted to see his father and mother now, and ask for their forgiveness. But they had exhausted their resources so completely in his behalf that there was no longer even a telephone in the house. There was no way to call them. Moreover, he wasn't even certain they would want to see him now. But he sent a telegram that read: "My train is passing through town this afternoon. If you want to see me, tie a white rag on the apple tree beside the tracks at the end of the street."

As the train came into the vicinity of his home town, tears began to fill the young man's eyes. He desperately wanted that rag—that sign of forgiveness—to be there. But he was afraid to look. He told the older man sitting beside him the whole story, then buried his face in his hands. The train rounded the bend. The apple tree came into view. The older man grabbed the young man's shoulders and lifted his face to the window. There, in all its splendor, was the apple tree with white rags flying from every single branch!

May you and I be ever ready to bring to our relationships such gifts of love and forgiveness, knowing, as we contemplate the Cross of Jesus Christ, that we have received that same incredible inheritance from God.

SOME QUESTIONS TO CONSIDER

1. If you just inherited $10 million, what would you do

with it?

2. Are there any superstitions that you, like Ichabod Crane, take seriously?
3. Can you think of something you did impulsively that you now regret?
4. If you could inherit a "Toad Hall" anywhere in the world where you would then live (but never sell), where would it be?
5. What are the three most important qualities of a close friend?
6. Was there anything Rat, Mole, and MacBadger could have done to "reform" Mr. Toad?

CHAPTER 11:

WHEN THE CLOCK STRIKES TWELVE: *CINDERELLA*

"Then the kingdom of heaven will be like this. Ten bridesmaids took their lamps and went to meet the bridegroom. Five of them were foolish, and five were wise. When the foolish took their lamps, they took no oil with them; but the wise took flasks of oil with their lamps. As the bridegroom was delayed, all of them became drowsy and slept. But at midnight there was a shout, 'Look! Here is the bridegroom! Come out to meet him.' Then all those bridesmaids got up and trimmed their lamps. The foolish said to the wise, 'Give us some of your oil, for our lamps are going out.' But the wise replied, 'No! there will not be enough for you and for us; you had better go to the dealers and buy some for yourselves.' And while they went to buy it, the bridegroom came, and those who were ready went with him into the wedding banquet; and the door was shut. Later the other bridesmaids came also, saying, 'Lord, lord, open to us.' But he replied, 'Truly I tell you, I do not know you.' Keep awake therefore, for you know neither the day nor the hour."

Matthew 25:1-13

Cinderella was Walt Disney's first full-length animated feature story since *Bambi*—released nearly eight years earlier. It has become one of the most beloved films in the Disney library, charmingly embellishing the traditional story recounted by Charles Perrault some three centuries ago.

Cinderella is a young girl whose father, a wealthy widower, remarries in order to provide his daughter a mother's love. But, alas, when the father himself dies, the girl's stepmother—Lady Tremaine—shows her true colors. She reduces Cinderella to the status of a kitchen-maid in her own chateau. She compels Cinderella to wait, hand-and-foot, on herself and her own two daughters, Cinderella's selfish step-sisters, Anastasia and Drizella.

Cinderella's only caring companions are the animals around the estate: a group of mice including one named Jaq, some birds, a horse named Major and a dog named Bruno. The one ill-tempered exception is a pampered and overfed cat named, appropriately enough, Lucifer.

Lucifer is forever making life miserable for Cinderella and her animal friends. One morning he tries to devour Gus, a chubby little newcomer among the mice. The cat traps Gus in a teacup on one of the breakfast trays Cinderella takes upstairs to serve her stepmother and stepsisters in their rooms. A scream from one of the girls' rooms alerts us that the mouse has been found. In the subsequent turmoil, Cinderella is accused of playing a trick. As punishment, her stepmother cruelly adds more burdens to her work load around the house.

Meanwhile, the King of the land is brooding over the fact that his one and only son has never married. How will the royal line continue? Together with the Grand Duke, he decides to organize a ball at the palace to which every eligible maiden will be invited.

Word reaches Cinderella's home. Lady Tremaine and her own two daughters become excited at the prospect. When Cinderella asks if she, too, may attend the ball, her stepmother slyly says, yes.....as long as she has "something presentable to wear" and she "gets all her work done". However, it immediately becomes evident that these are impossible conditions.

When Cinderella begins to patch up one of her mother's old dresses, she is summoned by the others to perform an inexhaustible list of chores.

When Cinderella sadly realizes that she will be unable to attend the ball, her animal friends come to the rescue. Using scraps that the stepsisters have discarded, they proceed to construct a beautiful gown. Cinderella is overjoyed when she discovers it and rushes down the stairs to accompany the others on this glorious adventure. But the stepsisters, seeing their discarded materials, tear Cinderella's dress to shreds—sending her weeping outside into the garden.

It is there and then that she encounters her fairy godmother, who uses her magical powers to give Cinderella a coach and a gown, complete with glass slippers, so that she can attend the ball after all. Remember just one thing, warns the fairy godmother. The spell will end—and everything will change again—when the clock strikes twelve.

Now, there's an even older story than *Cinderella* where the midnight hour plays a crucial role. It's the story Jesus told about a group of bridesmaids who—according to an ancient custom—went forth to meet a bridegroom and escort him to the home of his bride. Most oriental weddings like this were celebrated at night. Each bridesmaid carried a lamp, whose light was fueled by oil.

In this case, as Jesus told the story, the groom was delayed. So the bridesmaids stick their lamps in the ground and wait. Soon they begin to nod drowsily. Then they all fall asleep. Suddenly—when they are not expecting it—the clock strikes twelve, and the crucial announcement is made: "Look! Here is the bridegroom! Come out to meet him." *(Matthew 25:6)*

Here, I think, is the <u>first</u> thing both of these stories call to attention: <u>the unexpectedness of human experience.</u> Fate is fickle. We never quite know what's going to happen the next time the clock strikes twelve. One day Cinderella is a father's pride and joy. The next she is an abused kitchen-maid in her own home. Then one moment she is the victim of a cruel stepmother. The next she is the beneficiary of a fairy godmother. And at the midnight hour everything will change again.

The same is true for the bridesmaids in Jesus' parable. They have no idea when the bridegroom will arrive. One moment they are inattentive and asleep. Then the clock strikes twelve, and the scene becomes a flurry of activity.

It's an axiom of life that decisive moments can come at any hour. We're never so in control of our destiny that we can anticipate all its twists and turns. John Oman remarks somewhere that, while human beings make canals that go on a direct and unwavering course until they reach their goal, God made the rivers which meander from mountain springs, over plunging falls, through crooked valleys, in slow and devious ways to meet the sea. Our destinies are like the rivers. We are continually being surprised by the unexpected in life.

John Glenn, the first American to orbit the earth, came down from that historic adventure without a scratch. Then a few months later he slipped on a bar of soap in his bathroom and almost broke his neck.

A father waits anxiously in the maternity waiting room. When the nurse finally appears, he asks her frantically, "Tell me, is it a boy?" "Well," she answers, "the one in the middle is!"

Life is always a contest with the unexpected. We can never acquire enough education or self-confidence to protect us from life's crises and surprises.

It's interesting to remember that Jesus had a fundamentally different view of history than the prevailing philosophy of the Greco-Roman world of his day. The Greeks and Romans saw life as moving in cycles over vast expanses of time—

always recapitulating itself. Life, therefore, was really going nowhere, but simply turning round and round through long millenia—returning again and again to the same starting points and the same climaxes.

The interest in astrology and horoscopes is based on this same kind of ancient thinking. The rationale of studying the movement of the stars to predict the movement of human life is built on the assumption that life is just as cyclical as the stars—without freedom or responsibility, and therefore, without hope. The human being is a pawn instead of a person.

One of the major accomplishments of the Judeo-Christian tradition has been to break the grip of a predestined and essentially hopeless view of life. Life, as Jesus saw it, is not a treadmill of cycles, or star magnetisms, or foreordained chess moves. Life is an adventure. It moves, not along predetermined tracks, but into ever-new frontiers. And so it's always a contest with the unexpected. No calculations or manipulations will ever succeed in delivering us from having to deal with unexpected crises and surprises in our lives.

A man in Australia was a keen student of world affairs. Two or three years before the Second World War broke out, he concluded that such a war was inevitable. So he determined he would find the safest hide-out to which he could go. He studied a long time, and finally settled on a remote and sparsely populated island in the South Pacific. The name of the island was Guadalcanal. His hide-out turned out to be the center of one of human history's most terrific bombardments.

We can never escape the unexpected. It has an ironic way of seeking us out—wherever we are, however carefully we've tried to isolate ourselves from it. When the clock strikes twelve, anything can happen.

In Cinderella's case, midnight brings another new crisis, another turn of events. Thanks to her fairy godmother, she has gone to the royal ball. More than that, she has captured the Prince's heart. He has ignored every other maiden in his attraction to Cinderella. The King and the Grand Duke have observed his attentiveness with great satisfaction. They have jumped to the conclusion that their match-making scheme has been a complete success.

Then the clock strikes twelve. Caught off-guard, Cinderella remembers the warning she had received. She breaks away from the Prince in her effort to return home. He follows her and retrieves a glass slipper she has dropped on the staircase. When the twelfth chime of the clock sounds, Cinderella is back in her tattered clothes, far away from the palace. But she is spared one remnant of her enchanting evening. She still has the other glass slipper.

When the King learns that the nameless girl who has captured his son's heart has disappeared—leaving behind only a slipper—he orders the Grand Duke to search the land for the one whose foot will match that slipper. When news of this search reaches Cinderella's household, her stepsisters begin to speculate with excitement the possibility of fitting that slipper on one of their own feet, falsely qualifying for the honor of becoming the Prince's bride.

Cinderella herself becomes dreamily romantic at the news, recalling her night with the Prince. Lady Tremaine observes this unusual behavior and suspects what might have happened. In another of her cruel maneuvers, she locks Cinderella in her room in the attic.

Soon the Grand Duke and his assistant arrive at the chateau with the slipper. Each of the stepsisters is eager to prove that her foot is a perfect match for this glass footwear, but neither of them are able to cram into the slipper. It simply doesn't fit.

Something similar happens in the parable Jesus told. When the announcement is made that the bridegroom is about to arrive, it is the moment of truth. The bridesmaids all jump to their feet and tend to their lamps. But half of them are unable to arouse their flickering lights. They've failed to bring a sufficient supply of oil. So they try to borrow some from the other bridesmaids. But there's not enough for them to borrow. They scurry to try to buy some, but it's too late. By the time they return, the door is shut.

And here's a second truth in our stories: There are some things that just can't be borrowed. We have to provide them for ourselves. There are crucial moments in life when we cannot turn to someone else and claim what is hers alone to claim. We cannot wear a slipper that belongs only to Cinderella. We cannot claim oil that belongs only to another. Some things just can't be borrowed.

A little four-year-old boy was watching his modern grandmother prepare for bed. She removed her wig and her false eyelashes. She washed off her eyebrows and her lipstick. She put her dentures in a cup, then noticed how fascinated her grandson was, as he watched this whole process. "Grandma," he said. "Don't stop now. Take off your nose."

Well, there comes a point where things are no longer attachable and detachable. They are either a part of us, or they are not. And if they aren't, we can't expect to borrow them from someone else in a moment of crisis. These are the things that belong to the dominion of our character—things we have to develop for ourselves, if they are ever to become part of ourselves.

We may, for instance, borrow someone's possessions. But we cannot borrow his satisfaction. An old legend concerns a certain Oriental king who was very unhappy. He summoned a philosopher to ask for advice. The philosopher told him to seek out the most satisfied man in the kingdom, and to wear for a while his shirt. But when, after exhaustive investigation, they found the man, he was so poor that he didn't even have a shirt. Some things, like satisfaction, can't be borrowed. We have to find them for ourselves.

We may be able to borrow someone's tools or instruments. But we cannot borrow her talents. A Gaelic poem describes a mother playing a harp. Her children are gathered around her. They are entranced by the music. When she stops, the children pick up the harp and pluck the strings, trying to reproduce the music they have heard. But the sound is harsh and discordant. They ask their mother to show them the strings where the music is. She smiles and tells them that the music is indeed in the strings, but the power to draw it out is not hers to give them. She can help them, but they must seek and find it for themselves.

We may borrow someone's name, but not his spirit. We may borrow someone's acquisitions, but not her conscience. We may borrow someone's knowledge, but not his wisdom. We may borrow someone's circumstances, but not her faith. There are some things we have to find for ourselves, if they are ever to become a part of ourselves. In her book, *The Open Door,* Helen Keller wrote these words: "Our destiny is our responsibility, and without faith we cannot meet it competently." [12]

So here are Cinderella's stepsisters, contorting themselves in every possible fashion trying in vain to borrow something that does not belong to them—attempting to appropriate a slipper that fits Cinderella alone. Cinderella herself is locked in her attic room—unable to prove that the slipper belongs to her. At this critical moment she is shut off from her opportunity for happiness.

But wait! Her mouse friends, Gus and Jaq, have daringly managed to secure the key from Lady Tremain's pocket. They have made an arduous journey, carrying it painstakingly to the top of the stairs. But just as they are within inches of releasing Cinderella, Lucifer the cat appears and traps them outside the door. The birds, however, fly out the window to round up Bruno the dog, who arrives in the nick of time to dispatch Lucifer.

The Grand Duke is in the process of leaving when Cinderella rushes down the stairs to ask for her turn to try on the slipper. But just as the Grand Duke's assistant begins to walk in her direction, the malevolent stepmother causes him to trip, thereby shattering the glass slipper into a thousand pieces. Now it seems as if all is lost! But Cinderella calmly pulls from her pocket the one souvenir she still has from her romantic evening: the matching slipper. It fits perfectly! And so the story ends joyously with a royal wedding—which takes place, incidentally, when the clock strikes twelve, noon.

So also does Jesus's story about the bridegroom and the bridesmaids end happily with a wedding and a banquet to which the faithful are invited. Those who have conscientiously prepared themselves in the face of life's unexpectedness are those who can look forward to victory when the clock strikes twelve. For the victorious life is ultimately the virtuous life—the life that is loyal to responsibility and impelled by hope.

Here is the <u>third</u> lesson to be learned from our pair of parables: <u>We should always be preparing for the best</u>. This, admittedly, is something of a switch. Usually we're urged to prepare for the worst. We load ourselves with insurance for protection against disaster. Common sense recommends it. We spend billions on national defense, and seem miserly by comparison when asked to feed the hungry, educate the illiterate, and house the homeless.

But there is something self-defeating in the posture that expends all its energy bracing itself for the rainy day. It too easily loses sight of the sunny ones. If Cinderella had gone off to that royal ball focused on the fact that it would all be over when the clock struck twelve, she would never have been the kind of companion that so enchanted the Prince. The narrator describes Cinderella this way: "Through it all (she) remained ever gentle and kind. For with each dawn she found new hope that some day her dreams of happiness would come true."

God gave us the gift of life—not so that we should prepare for the worst, but that we should prepare for the best. To have faith in God is to trust in God's promise to ultimately bring opportunity out of crisis, victory out of defeat, Easter out of a Cross. It is to anoint the painful corners of human experience with the healing grace of God's love.

In his book, *A Gentle Thunder*, Max Lucado tells of a friend who had just returned from visiting Walt Disney World in Florida. This friend wanted to tell him about an experience that had been a highlight of their trip. His family happened to be inside Cinderella's Castle, the centerpiece of the Magic Kingdom. There was quite a crowd, and a beautiful young girl was playing the part of Cinderella. All the children pressed as close to her as they possibly could.

Lucado's friend happened to look in the opposite corner of the castle area. Standing there was a boy, about seven years old, holding the hand of his older brother. This young boy had a disfigured appearance. His face was deformed, and he was abnormally small in stature. He watched wistfully as Cinderella lavished her attention on all the other children.

Then something wonderful happened. Cinderella noticed this boy standing alone with his brother. She politely but firmly worked her way through the other children and walked over to him. She knelt down with a smile, and she kissed his face. The beaming smile he returned to her told the unmistakable story of his joy! [13]

So it is that God himself approaches you and me this very moment with both tenderness and affirmation. All God asks of us is that we be prepared—whatever the hour, whatever the circumstance—to receive those gifts of grace that are his eternal promise.

SOME QUESTIONS TO CONSIDER

1. What has been a truly unexpected surprise so far in your life?
2. If you had a fairy godmother, what would she offer to do for you?
3. If someone wanted to "borrow" one of your character traits, what do you suppose it would be?
4. What would have happened if the slipper had indeed fit Anastasia or Druzilla?
5. Do you spend more time imagining the best that might happen, or the worst that might happen?
6. Do you think Lady Tremaine and her daughters would be welcome in Cinderella's castle?

CHAPTER 12: WHAT ALICE FOUND IN WONDERLAND: *Alice in Wonderland*

On the first day of the week, when we met to break bread, Paul was holding a discussion with them; since he intended to leave the next day, he continued speaking until midnight. There were many lamps in the room upstairs, where we were meeting. A young man named Eutychus, who was sitting in the window, began to sink off into a deep sleep while Paul talked still longer. Overcome by sleep, he fell to the ground three floors below, and was picked up dead. But Paul went down, and bending over him took him in his arms, and said, "Do not be alarmed, for his life is in him." Then Paul went upstairs, and after he had broken bread and eaten, he continued to converse with them until dawn; then he left. Meanwhile they had taken the boy away alive and were not a little comforted.

Acts 20:7-12

At the beginning of his motion picture career, even before he came to Hollywood, Walt Disney created a short silent film entitled *Alice's Wonderland.* It featured a real six-year-old girl interacting with a cartoon world. It came to the attention of a New York distributor, who liked it sufficiently to sign a contract commissioning the Disney brothers to produce a series of shorts featuring the character, "Alice in

Cartoonland".

In later, more established years, the Disney Studio further adapted ideas from the Lewis Carroll books in animated shorts such as *Thru The Mirror* with Mickey Mouse and *Donald in Mathmagicland* with Donald Duck.

So it was not altogether unnatural for Disney to eventually make a full length animated version of the fictional classic, *Alice in Wonderland.* It was released in 1951.

The story begins on a beautiful day in an English garden. Alice's older sister is reading to her from a history book. But it's apparent that Alice's mind is somewhere else. She says to her little cat Dinah, "If I had a world of my own, everything would be nonsense. Nothing would be what it is, because everything would be what it isn't." With that clue as to what is to come, Alice suddenly spots a White Rabbit running full-speed on two feet. He's carrying an enormous pocket watch, and he's declaring aloud, "I'm late! I'm late! I'm late!"

Having never seen such a sight, Alice decides to follow him. When she pushes through a rabbit hole, she descends into a wonderland unlike anything she's ever experienced before. When she is unable to pursue the rabbit because she's too large for the door, the doorknob begins to talk to her. He invites her to try drinking the contents of a mysterious bottle. When she does this, Alice becomes a fraction of her former size. But the door is locked, and the key is on a table far too high for her to reach. So the doorknob invites her to try a cookie which immediately enlarges her far beyond her original size. Her tears of frustration at this point cause a veritable tidal wave at floor level. She discovers this when she samples more of the bottle and becomes so small she falls right into it.

Afloat now in the bottle, she is so tiny that she passes through the keyhole of the doorknob. She next encounters a Dodo and some other characters engaging in a Caucus Race, which consists in running around a rock in the middle of the sea, illogically trying to get dry. Then she spots the White Rabbit again and tries to catch up with him. Instead she encounters a strange pair of twins named Tweedledum and Tweedledee. They tell her the story of the Walrus and the Carpenter.

The White Rabbit appears again, and Alice chases after him. This time she catches up to him, and he sends her into his house. But she makes the mistake of eating another biscuit and becomes so large, she fills the house. The Dodo comes along and, because she is so large, he declares that she is a monster. He compels a lizard to climb down the chimney to get rid of her. But the soot causes Alice to sneeze, propelling the lizard up the chimney and out of sight. When the Dodo suggests burning the house down, Alice consumes a carrot, which makes her small again.

She runs after the White Rabbit, but loses him in a garden of flowers. Because she is so tiny, they tower over her. They begin asking her where she comes from and what kind of genus she might be. They finally conclude she is not their equal. She has no fragrance, no petals. She must be a weed, and they summarily dismiss her from the garden.

Lewis Carroll was the pen name of Charles Lutwidge Dodgson, who was a clergyman as well as a mathematician. There is penetrating social satire, as well as fantasy, in his stories of Alice. And surely one of the things he was satirizing was the arrogance that often surrounds size and status.

Alice's control of her situation in Wonderland often has to do with whether she's large enough or small enough. When she's too small, the flowers end up using the occasion to look down on her and call her a weed. They declare she couldn't possibly be their equal, and so they ostracize her from the garden. As she herself points out, if she were her normal size, she could pick all of them.

At a local baseball game, both the batter and the catcher were enormous brutes. The umpire at the plate happened to be a rather diminuitive fellow. The first ball was pitched. The umpire called out, "Strike one." The huge batter turned and glowered at him threateningly. The next pitch came, and this time the umpire called out, "Ball one." At this point the bruiser of a catcher turned and looked at him menacingly. Then came the third pitch. The umpire called out: "Two!" Both the batter and the catcher looked at him through squinted eyelids. "Two what?" they grunted. And the little umpire shrank into his padding and said, "Too close to call."

We live in a world where people are too often intimidated and stereotyped according to size, status, prestige, or some other measurement that convinces some people they are superior to others. It may be the size of their bank account, or the status of their ancestry, or the prestige of their occupation. Human history continues to be tarnished by countless examples of discrimination when such factors as race, gender, creed, disability, or age have been the excuse by which one group baldly discriminates against another.

Such was the case two thousand years ago in the society where the early Church came into being. The Roman empire was a patriarchal culture—one where some people owned others as slaves, and "might" claimed to make "right".

How amazing, therefore, is the scene described in the book of Acts where the apostle Paul is preaching in an upstairs room of a house in Troas. Unlike other social gatherings of that time and culture, the congregation included the rich and the poor, the master and the slave, Jews and Greeks, men and women, young and old.

Paul's sermons repeatedly reflected his conviction that "There is no longer Jew or Greek, there is no longer slave or free, there is no longer male and female; for all of you are one in Christ Jesus" *(Galatians 3:28).* In contrast to Lewis Carroll's "nonsense" and nightmarish world where Alice keeps encountering discourtesy and prejudice because she is different, Paul affirms that our differences are, in reality, gifts by which God has blessed us in order to serve one another. Instead of dividing us, our differences should help to complete us.

After Alice is banished by the flowers from their garden, her attention turns to a haughty caterpillar, who sits atop a gigantic mushroom, poses silly questions, and recites poetry. When Alice finally tells him she'd like to be larger than three inches tall, he declares huffily that he himself is exactly three inches tall. With that, he pops out of his garments and becomes a butterfly. His last words to Alice as he flies away are that both sides of the mushroom have size-changing properties.

So Alice changes size again—first becoming enormous, then returning to normal size. Her next encounter is with the Cheshire Cat, who appears and disappears at will, assuring Alice that everyone in this strange land is stark-raving mad. He tells her to ask the Mad Hatter or the March Hare about the White Rabbit. She finds the two of them, along with a drowsy Dormouse, engaged in a tea party. At first, she thinks they are celebrating someone's birthday, but they assure her this is an "unbirthday" party—just the opposite of what she would expect. A lot of silliness commences around the party table, with none of the characters responding directly to Alice's questions or taking her concerns seriously. Finally she decides to leave, saying she just doesn't have the time for such nonsense.

As if on cue, the White Rabbit appears again. Carrying his huge pocket watch, he complains that he has no time. He's late, so very, very late! The Mad Hatter grabs his watch, studies it a moment, and announces that it's two days slow. Then he dips it in the tea pot, opens it up and starts tinkering with its delicate machinery. Balance springs and pins pop out in every direction. Into the watch the Mad Hatter pours salt, butter, teaspoons, jam and lemon juice. When he closes the watch again, it begins to rumble and bounce as if it's going to erupt. The Mad Hatter uses an enormous mallet to smash it to bits.

Surely here's a <u>second</u> human obsession at which Lewis Carroll is poking fun in his books: <u>our anxiety over time</u>. Throughout her adventure Alice is in pursuit of a White Rabbit whose whole character is defined by his distress over being late. The characters at the tea party have no interest in celebrating a genuine anniversary. They are in a tizzy over un-birthdays. And when they get their hands on the White Rabbit's pocket watch, it becomes an excuse for their craziest conduct of all!

Our obsession with time often produces bizarre behavior. A teenager stayed out one night a couple of hours later than his curfew. As he arrived home, he turned off the car lights, cut the ignition, took his shoes off and did everything possible to slip into his room quietly. It was 2 A.M. As he walked down the hall, a light came on and his mother's voice was heard: "Is that you, son? What time is it?" "It's midnight, Mom," he answered. But just at that moment the cuckoo clock sounded two cuckoos. So he stood there and cuckooed ten more times!

When the late Herman Hickman was coaching football at Yale, he began the daily practice sessions at 4 P.M. The players frequently arrived late. Sometimes the entire squad wouldn't be assembled until 4:30. Hickman was frustrated about this loss of time. So, when all the players were finally present—whatever the time—he would turn the clock back to 4:00, and practice would begin.

We always seem to be thinking in terms of wasting a few minutes or saving them. Will Rogers wryly observed: "Half our life is spent trying to find something to do with the time we have rushed through life trying to save." However, our meticulous attention to the minutes may dull our appreciation for larger meanings in our destiny.

The greatest truths in life transcend all our clocks and calendars. When we're engaged in something that really matters to us, time seems to begin to lose its significance. A married couple was celebrating their 50th wedding anniversary. One of the guests remarked to the husband: "Fifty years! That's a long time with one person." The husband smiled and replied, "It would have been a lot longer without her."

All of us can remember certain moments in life—insights and experiences—whose value is so great that to measure them by the clock is irrelevant. Their power colors the rest of our life, and remains a source of strength and joy through all the vicissitudes of the years.

Surely it was like that for those people two thousand years ago who had come together in an upstairs room of a house in Troas to hear the apostle Paul. The average sermon today may last fifteen to thirty minutes. According to the book of Acts, Paul started his sermon on Sunday, went on through the night, and "continued to converse with them until dawn" the next day *(Acts 20:11)*. Luke, the author of Acts, doesn't share the specific content of Paul's sermon. It's sufficient for him to report that time seemed to dissolve in the presence of Paul's message.

In his book, *Wind, Sand and Stars*, the French writer and aviator St. Exupe'ry tells of some desert people who were visiting the French Alps. They were absolutely fascinated by a high waterfall. Their guide couldn't pull them away. They insisted, "We want to wait until it ends." Because water was so precious and rare in their experience, they couldn't conceive of a source of water going on forever. [14]

Nevertheless, some of life's greatest truths—above all, the promise of God's steadfast love, about which the apostle Paul preached—do indeed endure forever. And in their presence, our anxiety about time can begin to dissolve.

After the White Rabbit's watch is destroyed, Alice leaves the tea party and decides she no longer wants to follow the

White Rabbit. Instead, she now wants to go home. "No more nonsense!" she says. She wanders into a place called the Tulgey Woods, populated by a fantastic collection of birds and small animals. She discovers a path that looks promising. But as she walks along, she bumps into a dog who has brushes for a head and a tail, which he is using to erase the path.

Lost and all alone, Alice sits down and begins to cry. Why did she neglect her lessons and begin this adventure in the first place? Suddenly the Cheshire Cat reappears. When she tells him she wants to go home but can't find her way, he declares: "That's because you have no way. All ways here, you see, are the Queen's way!"

Alice next finds herself in the realm of the Queen of Hearts. There she first encounters some playing cards who are painting some roses red. It seems they planted white roses by mistake. The Queen insists on roses being red. Before they are able to finish, the Queen herself appears. She discovers the deception and gives the order, "Off with their heads!" And the unfortunate cards are dragged off to be executed.

When the Queen sees Alice, she challenges her to a game of croquet. Croquet, in the realm of the Queen of Hearts, turns out to be a drastically one-sided competition. Using a flamingo as a mallet and a hedgehog as a ball, the Queen misses her stroke. But knowing what's good for itself, the hedgehog begins rolling away toward the playing cards, which are arched into wickets. The cards do their best to manuver themselves to allow the hedgehog to roll through—with the exception of one unfortunate card who can't quite run fast enough. The Queen points to that card, and bellows, "Off with his head!"

These are conditions under which Alice has no chance. Furthermore, the Queen warns her, "If I lose my temper, you lose your head!" Things get even worse when the Cheshire

Cat reappears to impishly hook the flamingo's beak under the Queen's garment in such a way that her next shot topples her onto her own head. With red-faced fury, she blames Alice and orders her execution. The Queen's tiny and timid spouse asks her if Alice couldn't have a trial first.

This trial becomes a farce. None of the witnesses say anything relevant. The Queen insists that the sentence precede the verdict. It's a foregone conclusion that Alice will be executed. Suddenly Alice discovers a piece of mushroom still in her pocket, which she eats. Again her size increases twentyfold, and she is emboldened to call the Queen a pompous tyrant. Unfortunately, as she does so, she shrinks back to her former size. The Queen angrily recites her litany: "Off with her head!"

A hectic chase ensues that reintroduces the host of characters Alice has encountered in her adventures. Finally she comes back to the locked door, where the doorknob tells her she is asleep. She looks through the keyhole, and it's true. She is sleeping under a tree. This has all been a dream. "Wake up," she cries repeatedly, and the voice becomes that of her sister. Alice does wake up, back once again in the garden, where she is now wonderfully glad to be. And it's just in time for tea!

A <u>third</u> thing Lewis Carroll seems to be satirizing in the stories of Alice is the <u>pompous abuse of power.</u> The Queen of Hearts is a tyrant who rules with an iron fist. She punishes anyone who displeases her. She has the power to threaten death, and she wields that power ruthlessly.

There are different kinds of power in the world, and the real question is the purpose they ultimately serve. A hammer is a powerful tool for driving nails and smashing glass to pieces, but for the purpose of performing eye surgery, its power is virtually useless. A bomb is a powerful implement for blasting a crater and destroying a building, but for the purpose of comforting a crying child or planting a seed, it has no power whatsoever.

So we continually need to ask ourselves and our nations, What is the nature of our power? If our purpose is to reduce the known world to lifeless rubble, we have the power to do that at this very moment. But if our purpose is to heal the world, to reconcile it, to unite it, to turn human hearts from savagery and hate to civilization and cooperation.....then we need to ask ourselves if the power in which we trust—the power on which we spend most of our money and energy—is the kind of power that can truly accomplish that purpose.

In every arena of human relationships there are essentially two kinds of power: coercion and persuasion. They're not always mutually exclusive. We live in an imperfect world where we still need military strength and law enforcement to guard against chaos and crime. But in the struggle for the minds and hearts of persons, for the redemption of human life.....persuasion, rather than coercion, is the more potent power.

So the apostle Paul spent the whole of his converted life in places like Troas—preaching and teaching fellow human beings that the power that belongs to God's Kingdom is the power of love.

The report of his all-night session in that upstairs room contains an interesting anecdote. At about midnight a young man named Eutychus, who was sitting in the window, nodded off and fell asleep. Indeed, he fell out the window, dropped three stories, and was pronounced dead. But Paul immediately interrupted his sermon, went downstairs, and restored the young man's life—or perhaps determined that he wasn't really dead after all.

What a contrast to the Queen of Hearts, whose only power was the power to threaten death! Paul represented God's power to restore life. Here is the choice of Kingdoms that confronts every one of us every hour. One is the rule of coercion. The other is the rule of persuasion. One acts to harm the blunderer. The other seeks to heal the broken. One threatens our mortality. The other ultimately promises us immortality. One resembles the realm of the fictitious Queen of Hearts, whom Alice called a pompous tyrant. The other reveals the realm of a faithful King of Hearts, whom Jesus called our heavenly Father.

During the First World War—so much of which was fought in muddy trenches—two soldiers looked out across no-man's-land. The younger one saw the barbed wires, the mudholes, the broken bodies of men—all the mad evidence of human hostility and the abusive power unleashed by coercion. "Captain," he asked, "where is God in all this?" At that moment two non-combatant stretcher-bearers climbed over the top and moved out under enemy fire to pick up a wounded soldier. And the captain said, "Look, son, there God is. There goes God now."

God's realm—God's kingdom—is reflected wherever compassion has a human face. Alice encountered a Wonderland that turned out to be a nightmare from which she longed to go home. The Cross of Christ has revealed a kingdom of wonder and promise and grace where you and I can be at home forever.

SOME QUESTIONS TO CONSIDER

1. What ideal size would you like to be (height, weight, etc.)?
2. Does Alice seem to have more problems when she is little or when she is large?
3. Can you describe an experience when "time stood still"?
4. Do you know someone like the White Rabbit, who is

always late?

5. Did your favorite teacher rely mostly on coercion or persuasion?
6. Is there a world leader today like the Queen of Hearts?

CHAPTER 13: YOU AND YOUR SHADOW: *PETER PAN*

Now many signs and wonders were done among the people through the apostles. And they were all together in Solomon's Portico. None of the rest dared to join them, but the people held them in high esteem. Yet more than ever believers were added to the Lord, great numbers of both men and women, so that they even carried out the sick into the streets, and laid them on cots and mats, in order that Peter's shadow might fall on some of them as he came by. A great number of people would also gather from the towns around Jerusalem, bringing the sick and those tormented by unclean spirits, and they were all cured.

Acts 5:12-16

Originally created as a stage production, J. M. Barrie's *Peter Pan* has had a variety of incarnations in the theater, in books, and in motion pictures. In 1939 Walt Disney acquired the rights to produce an animated film of the story. But nearly a decade and a half passed before the Disney version was released. It was an immediate success.

The story begins in the London home of the Darling family, where Mr. Darling is in a dither preparing for a social engagement. While getting dressed, he discovers that his cuff links and shirt have been appropriated by his two sons, John and Michael, who are using them as a treasure and a map while pretending to be pirates. They are enacting one of the bedtime stories that their older sister, Wendy, has been telling them about Peter Pan, the boy who never grows up. Mr. Darling is furious. He declares that such "poppycock" is harmful to their minds. He announces that this will be the last night they can all sleep together in the nursery. Tomorrow Wendy will be moved to another room.

After colliding with Nana—the large, gentle dog who acts as the children's nursemaid—Mr. Darling marches her outside and ties her up. Finally father and mother leave for their party. As they disappear down the street, we spot an elfish figure on the roof. It is Peter Pan himself, accompanied by the tiny pixie, Tinker Bell. The two of them enter the nursery quietly. They're looking for Peter's shadow, which Wendy retrieved earlier from Nana and locked in a drawer.

When they finally find the shadow, it proves to be an elusive entity indeed. It leaps all over the room before Peter can pounce on it, waking Wendy in the process. She proceeds to sew the fugitive shadow onto the soles of his shoes.

Now, lest we dismiss this narrative about a fugitive shadow too quickly, let's recall an even older story about a shadow and someone named Peter. It's found in the New Testament book of Acts. The shadow in question belonged to the apostle Peter, prominent leader in the early Church. Indeed, his influence was so profound that it is reported "that they even carried out the sick into the streets, and laid them on cots and mats, in order that Peter's shadow might fall on some of them as he came by" *(Acts 5:15)*.

We're certainly aware of the power of celebrity—how fans can connect mystically with a rock singer's scarf or a movie star's autograph. So it shouldn't surprise us that the shadow of a man of such spiritual stature as the apostle Peter should be thought to have healing properties. Similar accounts have been told of other personalities. When Mahatma Gandhi was alive, people would go to great lengths to try to manuver themselves so that his shadow might fall upon them.

Yet, when we stop to think about it, it's not only the famous who have shadows. The same thing can be said of you and me. Indeed, here is the very first thing we ought to acknowledge: Every one of us casts a shadow that has an impact on other lives, for good or ill. We can no more keep from exerting some kind of influence than we can keep from casting a shadow on a sunny day.

Peter Pan's shadow affected—in one way or another—the whole Darling household. The apostle Peter's shadow influenced the whole family of the Christian Church.

When a stone is dropped into a pool of water, ripples begin reaching out in widening circles until they finally touch the shore. In the same manner, we cannot participate in the pool of life without causing tiny ripples of influence that begin to move toward the very shores of eternity.

As long as we stand in the light of life, the shadow of our influence—whether we're conscious of it or not—is continually sending out silent, invisible forces that touch other people's lives—shaping their thoughts, molding their opinions, lifting them up in inspiration or pulling them down in depression. Likewise, we ourselves are affected more than we know by the shadows of other people—what they say and do and are—the invisible pull of their lives upon ours. They teach us lessons and cast impressions.

Oliver Wendell Holmes once said that he probably would have entered the ministry except for the fact that so many clergypeople looked like undertakers. For those of us who entered that calling anyway, one of the most interesting aspects of the ministry is the continual discovery that people are influenced by the most unpredictable things. There are times when someone may express appreciation, and it's a marvelous surprise to learn that you've been a positive influence in somebody's life without even knowing it. On the other hand, there are times when someone may misunderstand or misinterpret something you've said or done, and the influence seems negative despite the best of intentions. The effect of our influence often eludes our most careful calculations.

There's a silly story about a maiden lady who bought a parrot. It turned out that the only two words the bird could say were, "Let's neck. Let's neck." It so happened that the minister next door had a parrot that had learned to say, "Let's pray. Let's pray." After consultation, the parrot owners decided to put the birds in a common cage for a few days—hoping that the influence of the minister's parrot might teach the lady's parrot a more fitting phrase. When they put the birds together, her parrot said, "Let's neck." And the minister's parrot said, "My prayers have been answered."

So it is that our influence is largely unpredictable. It's not something we can turn on and off intentionally, and engineer all the consequences. Parents sometimes mistakenly think they can do that. They resolve one day to put on a good example for their children. They offer a spurt of intentional behavior to convince themselves they are good parents. Then they relax and congratulate themselves that they have been a positive influence in their children's lives. And, in some small, sporadic way, perhaps it's true.

But the largest part of a parent's influence is unconscious. It's the day-by-day shadow a parent casts upon a child's life—the undergirding spirit of that relationship that either fulfills or contradicts the conscious efforts to prove one's self a good parent. Someone has said that children are natural mimics. They act like their parents in spite of every effort to teach them good manners.

A family was entertaining dinner guests, and the mother

asked her six-year-old daughter to offer the grace before the meal. The child seemed confused and asked what she should say to God. The mother, somewhat embarrassed, said, "Just pray like Mommy prays." So the little girl bowed her head and solemnly declared: "O Lord, why did I invite these boring people on a hot day like this?"

Luther Burbank once offered this observation: "If we had paid no more attention to our plants than we have to our children, we would now be living in a jungle of weeds." A lot of young people today are living in a jungle of aimlessness and confusion and cynicism, primarily because they have lived under shadows that hurt instead of healed.

Shadows—influence—for good or for ill.....you and I are sending them into the stream of humanity constantly.

As Wendy reattaches that shadow to Peter Pan, she tells him that this is her last night in the nursery. Peter is horrified. That means she will no longer be telling stories about him. He offers to take her to the island of Never Land, where she will never grow up. The boys also wake up and want to go to Never Land too. So Peter teaches the three of them how to fly, with the aid of a little pixie dust.

No sooner do they arrive in Never Land than they are under attack by a band of pirates led by the scurrilous Captain Hook. Hook, whose amputated hand had been tossed by Peter to a crocodile long ago, lives for revenge. Peter instructs Tinker Bell to escort the children to his hideout while he diverts the pirates. But Tinker Bell has become jealous of Peter's attention to Wendy. She hurries ahead to instruct the Lost Boys—Peter's devoted followers—to attack Wendy. They shoot her down, but Peter arrives in time to scold Tinker Bell for her treachery and to banish her, at least temporarily.

John and Michael immediately feel right at home in Never Land. They join the Lost Boys on a hunting expedition, but they all end up being captured by the resident Indian tribe. The chief accuses them of kidnapping his daughter Tiger Lily. Meanwhile, what Peter and Wendy discover is that Tiger Lily has really been abducted by Captain Hook and his sidekick Mr. Smee. They are attempting to force information from her about the location of Peter Pan's hideout. Fortunately, Peter is able to save Tiger Lily and send Hook scurrying from the hungry crocodile.

Later Hook learns that Tinker Bell has been banished by Peter Pan and sends Mr. Smee to retrieve her. Playing upon her jealousy, he persuades her that the pirates are planning to leave the island. He slyly tells her that he would like to take Wendy with him, so that Tinker Bell and Peter could be happy together again. Hook only needs to know where they are hiding. Tinker Bell falls for his deception and reveals the location of the hideout. Hook promptly locks her in a lantern and leads the pirates to the place in question. They succeed in capturing everyone but Peter. For him they leave a bomb, which has been disguised as a present from Wendy.

Now, this suggests a <u>second</u> thing that should be said about that shadow of influence every one of us casts: <u>it is irrevocable</u>. Once it has been exerted, it can never be recalled.

Peter Pan's invitation to take Wendy to Never Land cast a shadow that sparked Tinker Bell's jealousy, just as the shadow of Tinker Bell's jealousy set loose a wave of pirate tyranny. However much she would regret it, once Tinker Bell had revealed the location of Peter's hideout, there was no way to conceal it again.

A person can change her business, her vocation, her residence, her nationality, even her name. But the influence that has gone out from her life into other lives cannot be changed. A person may even change himself. He may make the decision to do everything he can to become a better influence. But he can never recall the influence that has already helped to fashion other lives and the influence of those lives, extending in an invisible, intangible way through all of space and time.

Do you remember Benjamin Franklin's adage? "For want of a nail, the horseshoe was lost. For want of a shoe, the horse was lost. For want of a horse, the rider was lost." Our shadow has a way of extending an influence far beyond our comprehension. A harsh thought may lead to a harsh word, which may lead to a harsh attitude, which may lead to a harsh deed, which may lead to a harsh relationship. Just such alienation and suspicion and hostility can be the catalysts which lead to stereotypes and hatred and war.

The silliest presumption a person can have is that he can control the consequences of his influence. The truth is that everything we do has a quality to it that is something like immortality. It lives on, even after we ourselves are gone from the face of the earth.

The idea of a Judgment Day at the end of history is really a theological reminder that the full consequences of our influence have yet to be completed, even after our lives on earth are done. Not until the end of history itself can a person know how his influence is registered in the total life of the human race. Until then, our shadow—our personal measure of influence—unfolds in its mysterious, invisible, irrevocable way.

The Darling children and the Lost Boys have become the captives of the pirates when Peter discovers the package that, unknown to him, conceals a bomb. Fortunately a penitent Tinker Bell has successfully broken out of the lantern and rushed to the rescue. Putting herself in peril, she pushes away the bomb just seconds before it explodes. Peter is able to revive her while assuring her that she means more to him than anything in the world.

Together they fly to the pirate ship, where a comical battle ensues between the boys and the buccaneers. Peter and Captain Hook square off, and Hook makes Peter agree he will not use his ability to fly. When Peter gets the upper hand anyway, Hook treacherously attempts to slay him in the back. But Peter's quick evasion sends the pirate splashing into the water. The children triumph, and our last glimpse of Captain Hook is that of a panicked swimmer being eagerly pursued by his nemesis, the crocodile.

Tinker Bell sprinkles the pirate ship with pixie dust. It soars into the sky and returns to London, where the Darling children are at home again. When Mr. and Mrs. Darling return from their party, they are alarmed to find that Wendy's bed is empty. But then they find her sleeping by the window. She awakens and begins to tell of their adventures, pointing out the window to the cloud-like shadow of the pirate ship. As he studies it, Mr. Darling's crusty skepticism crumbles. With a look of wonder on his face, he confesses to his family that he has the feeling that he has seen that ship before.....a long time ago when he, too, was very young.

There's a <u>third</u> thing that should be said about our shadow of influence: <u>The kind of shadow we cast has to do with the kind of light in which we stand.</u>

That light is determined by the dreams that shine upon our lives, the sources of inspiration and truth that guide us. If the dreams by which we live are dim and dysfunctional, that quality will be reflected in our shadow. But if our lives are illuminated by dreams that embrace life's highest possibilities, the shadow we cast will carve silhouettes in that quality of light.

The dreams of Peter Pan and the Darling children revolved around the wonder of life, the magic of childhood imagination, the importance of fair play, the ethics of loyalty and love. Those dreams were finally reawakened in their father as well.

Such dreams and values can deepen the relationship between any parent and child.

A little girl happened to accidentally break a vase that was a cherished heirloom. Because she knew how valuable it was, she began to cry when she saw it in pieces on he floor. Her mother came running into the room. Expecting the worst, the girl was surprised to see, not anger, but relief on her mother's face. "I thought you were hurt," said her mother, gathering the child in her arms.

Looking back on that event, the girl, now a young woman, made this observation: "That was the day I discovered that I was the family treasure!" Would that all homes could be filled with such discoveries and such dreams!

On the other hand, the dreams of Captain Hook and his crew revolved around the quest for revenge, the practice of treachery, the norm of foul play. Visions of plunder and loot are the dreams by which a pirate lives, and the shadow he casts is sordid and dangerous.

Human history itself is populated with both Peter Pans and pirates, champions of childhood innocence as well as scurvy villains of every stripe.

But the wonderful news is that you and I can choose the dreams that will illuminate our lives. Those dreams can be either demeaning or inspiring. On the one hand, we can live by visions of selfishness and greed. We can dedicate our energies to hallucinations of prestige and power. We can even allow our days to revolve around the latest fad and whatever happens to be popular practice. Or, on the other hand, we can seek to stand where the light is pure and true.

The apostle Peter stood alongside one who, for two thousand years, has been called "the light of the world" *(John 8:12)*. Indeed, no image may better describe Jesus the Christ than the image of light. The New Testament does it repeatedly: "The fruit of the light is found in all that is good and right and true" *(Ephesians 5:9)*. "In him was life, and the life was the light of all people" *(John 1:4)*." "It is the God who said, 'Let light shine out of darkness.' who has shone in our hearts to give the light of the knowledge of the glory of God in the face of Jesus Christ" *(2 Corinthians 4:6)*. His teachings illuminate the meaning of righteousness. His ministry interprets the power of truth. His gift of himself on the Cross is a window through which the love of God shines.

And Peter stood directly in that light. As his friend and disciple, Jesus had entrusted his gospel to Peter. That gospel was the "good news" of the Kingdom of God—the dream of life animated by God's rule. And that dream was not a fantasy, but an ever-present reality. Its evidence is forever to be found in the shadows of lives like Peter, whose influence God uses to heal brokenness, to forgive sin, to fill emptiness, to reconcile estrangement, to sanctify every moment and experience with the mercy of an eternal grace.

It was a May morning in nineteenth century Scotland when a baby was born into a Christian family and named Jamie after his grandfather. He was the ninth child in that home. But when he was only seven, one of his teenage brothers was killed in a tragic skating accident. Jamie's mother went into a state of deep depression. With childhood innocence, Jamie thought he might be able to comfort her by playing the part of his brother. So he put on his brother's clothes and imitated his special whistle. At that tender age he became an actor. Gradually his mother sensed the compassion he was trying to communicate, and she was able to cope with her grief.

It was not surprising that Jamie took a fancy to drama and literature in school. He eventually became a writer himself—contributing articles to magazines and composing novels. But his greatest love was writing plays, and several of them were quite successful.

He always had a special rapport with children, no doubt enhanced by his unique ability to elevate and lower his eyebrows separately in opposite directions. Once he went on a walk in the woods with a pair of children and led them to a tree with a hollow trunk. Inside they found a peapod. When the children opened it, they discovered it contained a letter, which Jamie said was a fairy story he would read to them. They were enchanted.

The story for which we know Jamie best is *Peter Pan.* Since its first performance in 1904, it has been in virtually continuous performance all over the world. J. M. Barrie—creator of the boy who never grew up—himself never had a child of his own. But, in his later years, he became the protector and champion of many children. And at the end of his life, he made a wonderful gift. He bestowed all the rights and royalties from his most famous and successful creation, *Peter Pan,* to the Great Ormond Street Hospital for Sick Children in London. To this day, the shadow of J.M. Barrie's influence has touched—not only the young in spirit everywhere—but also countless lives of children whom that distinguished institution has helped to comfort and to heal.

So, too, may the shadows of your life and mine ultimately be an influence for good in the balances of eternity. To that end, may we stand firmly in the light of God's love.....the light that never fails.....the love that never ends.

SOME QUESTIONS TO CONSIDER

1. What three people, outside of your family, have greatly influenced your life?
2. Do you know a great story-teller like Wendy?
3. Can you remember an occasion when something you said was completely misunderstood?

4. What advice would you give Tinker Bell when she is the prisoner of Captain Hook?
5. If you could stop aging at any part of your life, how old would you want to remain?
6. Should Mr. Darling change his mind and let Wendy stay in the nursery after all?

CHAPTER 14: THE GENTLE ART OF JUDGING OTHERS: *LADY AND THE TRAMP*

"Do not judge, and you will not be judged; do not condemn, and you will not be condemned. Forgive, and you will be forgiven; give, and it will be given to you. A good measure, pressed down, shaken together, running over, will be put into your lap; for the measure you give will be the measure you get back."

He also told them a parable: "Can a blind person guide a blind person? Will not both fall into a pit? A disciple is not above the teacher, but everyone who is fully qualified will be like the teacher. Why do you see the speck in your neighbor's eye, but do not notice the log in your own eye? Or how can you say to your neighbor, 'Friend, let me take out the speck in your eye,' when you yourself do not see the log in your own eye? You hypocrite, first take the log out of your own eye, and then you will see clearly to take the speck out of your neighbor's eye."

Luke 6:37-42

Walt Disney's *Lady and The Tramp* is based on an unpublished original story by Ward Greene. This was a new approach for the studio, whose previous animated features had been linked to familiar novels and famous fairy tales. *Lady and The Tramp* was also the first animated feature to be made in the wide-screen format of CinemaScope.

The title characters are a pair of dogs in an early twentieth century American city. It is Christmas when the story begins in an affluent neighborhood. A husband—known to us as "Jim Dear"—presents a hat box as a present to his young wife—known as "Darling". Instead of a hat, however, it contains a beautiful spaniel puppy, who is promptly named Lady.

When Lady is left alone downstairs that evening as the couple retires to their bedroom, she uses every trick in the canine book to get upstairs and gain a place at the foot of their bed. She eventually succeeds. As she falls asleep in that position, the image of a young puppy transforms with time into that of Lady, a mature young dog.

The day arrives when Lady receives a collar and a license, of which she is enormously proud. She shows them to her neighborhood friends—two older dogs—a Scottish terrier named Jock and a bloodhound named Trusty, who has lost his sense of smell. They congratulate her enthusiastically. It's not long after that when Lady senses something different is happening in her home. When she describes the signs, Jock and Trusty inform her that her mistress Darling must be expecting a baby.

At this point, Tramp appears on the scene. He's a footloose, unlicensed dog from the other side of the tracks. He has wandered into this expensive neighborhood after fleeing the dog catcher. Upon hearing that Lady's owners are expecting a baby, he cynically predicts that Lady will lose their affection. As he says, "A human heart has only so much room for love and affection. When a baby moves in, the dog moves out." With that, Jock and Trusty angrily chase Tramp off the property, dismissing him as a worthless scamp.

Soon the baby arrives. But, contrary to Tramp's prediction, Jim Dear and Darling continue to love Lady. Indeed, Lady herself comes to love the baby. However, the domestic tranquillity is shattered when Jim Dear and Darling have to leave town for a few days. They prevail upon Aunt Sarah to run the house. Aunt Sarah arrives with two Siamese cats, who turn out to be little short of diabolical. With Aunt Sarah elsewhere in the house, they make a shambles of the living room while trying to catch the pet canary and the goldfish. Lady does her best to protect the premises, but when Aunt Sarah discovers the mess, the cats pretend to be wounded. Aunt Sarah immediately blames Lady for the disaster and carries her off to the pet store to have her muzzled.

Aunt Sarah is guilty of a common transgression—one against which Jesus warned you and me: "Do not judge, and you will not be judged; do not condemn, and you will not be condemned." *(Luke 6:37)*

Jesus wasn't suggesting that there is no place for judgment in life. After all, none of us can maneuver through a single day without making priority judgments about the use of our time and energy and resources. When we study the context, we find that Jesus was talking specifically about our negative judgments of other people—our criticisms and condemnations—and the temptation we have to put ourselves in the role of God.....to think that our judgments are the final ones. He was cautioning us to never forget three things that ought to temper our judgments with wisdom and gentleness.

In the first place, he cautions us to remember that there's always so much that we don't know about the one we're judging. When Aunt Sarah confronts the evidence of misbehavior, she doesn't even consider the possibility that her beloved cats could in any way be responsible. The guilty party must be this dog to whom she has just been introduced.

Aunt Sarah is not alone in this transgression. Jock and Trusty, Lady's friends, are quick to judge Tramp as a worthless mongrel from the other side of the tracks. Tramp himself is quick to judge Lady's owners as fickle human beings who will ignore her after the birth of their baby. Many of us seem determined to set speed records when leaping to conclusions about others.

There's always a great deal we don't really comprehend about another person—even someone we think we know best. No matter how much we know about a person, there's always something that remains unknown. That's why our closest relationships are limited to so few, and why surface attraction is a poor foundation for judgment. A young couple broke off their engagement to each other with the comment: "It was love at first sight—but then we took another look."

A colleague of mine told of once being passed abruptly by a friend, without even a nod of recognition. He judged that he was being deliberately snubbed, until later he learned that his friend was slowly becoming blind. I remember once seeing an acquaintance weaving down the street, and judging that he must be intoxicated. Then later I learned the man was suffering from a disease of the inner ear that affected his sense of balance.

Haven't we all had experiences like that? Our judgment proved wrong because we didn't really know enough. Unfortunately that didn't stop us from passing judgment. That familiar old Indian prayer deserves to be laminated in our minds: "Great Father, never let me judge another until I have walked in his moccasins."

Consider what would happen if we could change places, for a week or two, with the person we employ or who employs us or who is unemployed, with the person who delivers our mail or collects our garbage, with the person who bags our groceries or teaches our children, with the person who waits on our table or parks our car, with the person who lives in a high-crime neighborhood or in a convalescent home, with the person who just lost her husband, her child, her house, her savings, or the person who never had any of them in the first place. I guarantee that our judgments would be different.

We might begin to feel more acutely the stress under which other people live.....people who are ensnared in marriages that are abusive, people who are crippled by disappointments in their chosen careers, people who are anxious about children who have taken a wrong turn, people who carry the burden of unseen injury and unsuspected despair.

In judging other people, we should heed Jesus' caution that there's always so much about them that we don't really know.

So, in the story of *Lady and The Tramp*, Aunt Sarah has muzzled Lady, blaming her for a calamity for which Aunt Sarah's own cats were responsible. Distressed by the muzzle, Lady breaks loose and begins running down the street. Three mean-looking dogs begin to chase her and corner her against a fence. Suddenly Tramp appears and chases away the bullies.

Lady and the Tramp's next stop is the zoo, where Tramp persuades a hardworking beaver that the muzzle could be a useful tool for pulling logs. The beaver uses his strong teeth to bite through the muzzle strap, setting Lady free. Tramp then introduces Lady to his favorite haunts around the town. This includes a stop in the alley outside Tony's Italian Restaurant, where Tramp can always count on a free meal. Tonight it's spaghetti and meatballs, with Tony and his cook Joe serenading the two dogs. It's clear that a canine romance is blossoming.

When morning comes, Tramp invites Lady to join him in his carefree, unlicensed lifestyle. But Lady begins thinking about home and the baby she should be near. She needs to return to where she belongs. Tramp reluctantly agrees to escort her back to her neighborhood. On the way, however, he spots a chicken coop. He can't resist showing her the fun of chasing the hens, sending them into a frenzy. Unfortunately, the commotion attracts the dog-catcher. Lady is the dog he catches.

In the dog pound Lady meets a colorful assortment of characters. A quartet of them—a bulldog, a dachshund, a Russian wolfhound, and a chihuahua—wail mournfully their version of "Home, Sweet Home". Another of the dogs at the pound is a furry flirt named Peg. She sings a song that informs Lady of Tramp's roguish reputation. It seems that in the past he's had quite a few female friends among the canine set.

Because Lady has a license, it isn't long before Aunt Sarah comes to claim her. She takes Lady home and chains her outdoors to a doghouse. When Tramp comes to see her, remorseful for having chased the hens and causing such trouble, Lady explodes in anger. It becomes clear that the source of her irritation is what she has learned about Tramp from the other dogs at the dog pound. In the past he's been quite a playboy with the ladies. So Lady judges his professed affection for her as insincere.

And this suggests a <u>second</u> word of caution Jesus would bring to our judgments. When we judge someone else, <u>we cannot judge him solely and exclusively on the basis of something in his past</u>. Rather, like a drama, we have to wait and see how everything is going to turn out.

A married couple were entertaining some friends in their home one evening. Their seven-year-old daughter Margaret was playing quietly in the corner of the room. The adult conversation turned to the topic of hair color and whether it relates to a woman's disposition. One of the guests made the statement: "I think blondes have the nicest personalities."

"No," said another, "I think redheads are by far the most congenial."

"Brunettes," insisted a third, "are certainly the friendliest."

Then one of them looked over at Margaret and asked her,

"What about you Margaret? What do you think?"

"I think you should ask Mommy," said the little girl. "She's been all three, so she should know!"

We can no more judge a person's character than we can judge a person's hair color solely and exclusively on the basis of something in that person's past.

Some years ago, Coach Joe Paterno and his Penn State football team were playing for the national championship against Alabama in the Sugar Bowl. They probably would have won, but they had a touchdown called back because there was a twelfth man on the field. After the game, Paterno was asked to identify the player. "It's only a game," he said. "I have no intention of ever identifying the boy, and branding him forever with that one mistake."

There have been moments in the past when every person has been at his worst. You've had those moments. I've had those moments. Maybe they've been months, even years, instead of moments. But there are other moments. The crucial thing is where it all comes out in the end. We have to see the whole person before we can truly judge him. That includes the future possibility as well as the past performance.

One of my professors at Yale Divinity School, Bill Muehl, was once visiting the Virginia home of an illustrious colonial family. As he was given a tour of the residence, he happened to notice an old rifle above the fireplace. He asked whether he might take it down and examine it. He was told that it wouldn't be safe. "You see, it's all loaded and primed to fire," said his elderly hostess. "My great-grandfather kept it there in constant readiness against the moment when he might strike a blow for the freedom for the colonies." Dr. Muehl remarked that her great-grandfather must therefore have died before the Revolution. "Oh no," she replied. "He lived to a ripe old age and died in 1802, but he never had confidence in George Washington. You see, he knew Washington as a boy and didn't believe he could ever lead an army!"

One doesn't judge the character of George Washington solely by something from his boyhood—any more than one judges Abraham Lincoln by his business failures or his election losses. What is the whole picture? What will be the final perspective? That's the important question.

And so it is with *Lady and The Tramp.* As Tramp turns away—rejected by Lady for what she has learned about his past—a large, menacing-looking rat slithers onto the scene. It climbs up the side of the house and in through the window that leads to the baby's room. Unable to break the chain that holds her back, Lady begins barking frantically. Hearing her, Tramp turns back to see what could be the matter. She tells him about the rat.

Tramp rushes into the house and up the stairs to the baby's room. There he disposes of the rat, but in the process tips over the baby's crib. Aunt Sarah hears the baby crying, comes into the room and sees Tramp. Not noticing the remains of the rat, she makes another rash judgment. She assumes Tramp has been attacking the baby. She immediately calls the dog-catcher to dispose of Tramp, whom she judges to be vicious and dangerous.

After the dog-catcher leaves the house with Tramp in his horse-drawn wagon, Jim Dear and Darling return home. Lady, who by this time has broken loose from her chain, leads them to the dead rat. All of them now realize what really happened. Jim Dear calls the pound, but there's no answer. Jock and Trusty decide they must pursue the dog-catcher's wagon and stop it before something drastic happens to Tramp. Trusty—whose sense of smell has been supposed to be lost—amazes Jock by picking up the scent. They finally succeed in catching up with the wagon. But the frightened horses bolt, overturning the wagon. Jim Dear, Darling and Lady reach the scene in a taxi and discover Tramp unharmed. However, they also discover the inert body of Trusty, upon whom the wagon has fallen.

The final scene takes us back to where we began. It's Christmas once again. But this Christmas Tramp is a member of the family, proudly wearing a collar. And there are four puppies under the tree. Three of them look just like Lady looked on a previous Christmas. And one of them is a miniature version of Tramp. A couple of visitors come to call. It's Jock and Trusty, whom we presumed to be dead. In fact, it turns out he was only wounded and now wears a cast on his leg. So the Christmas celebration is complete, with more joy at the end than had ever been there before.

And this suggests the third word of caution Jesus would bring to our judgments. He would remind us that the final judgment always belongs to God alone. But that's not just a warning. Ultimately it represents a promise.

"Do not judge, and you will not be judged; do not condemn, and you will not be condemned. Forgive, and you will be forgiven." *(Luke 6:37)*

God has promised to judge us no more harshly than we judge one another. Indeed, God's judgments are forever tempered by forgiveness and mercy. Just as the lives of people we judge can sometimes be vitally affected by those judgments, so do our own destinies hang by the very thread of God's judgment upon us. Whenever we are tempted to judge another person, we need to remember the wondrous mystery of God's purpose—that goodness can sometimes come out of evil, that strength can sometimes come out of weakness, that victory can sometimes come out of defeat. The seeds of transformation may be planted through the mercy of grace.

It is the stubborn glory of Christian faith to believe that, in spite of all the sins of the past, there is always hope in the future. That's because, ultimately, the only Judge to whom we are all finally accountable is God himself. God is not a God who looks at us with logs in his eyes, but a God who sees purely—even into the darkest secrets in our hearts.

Yet God is a God to whom we can turn for the mercy of grace. And if that comforts us when others judge us wrong or weak or worthless, it should also caution us—as Jesus cautions us—to temper our own judgments of other people with wisdom and gentleness. We should be willing to forgive, for we ourselves are in need of forgiveness.

Years ago in one of our large cities there was an argument between a father and son whose relationship had become strained. Angry words were exchanged. When the boy stomped out of the house, the door was slammed. After the boy had been gone for several days, the father began to be worried. When the boy was gone for several weeks, the father was devastated. He began spending every spare minute searching the streets of the city for his son. Finally, in a last desperate effort to find him, he put an ad in every newspaper in town that read like this: "Dear John, please meet me in front of the flagpole in the park at noon on Sunday. As for me, all is forgiven. I love you. Your father."

On Sunday at noon standing beside that flagpole in the park was that father's son.....as well as 15 other young men named John—sons who were hungry for the forgiveness and love of their own fathers.

God gave a gift to a world that is too quick to judge people by their past sins and their unknown proclivities. That gift is Christmas itself—the birth and incarnation of a life who revealed God's final judgment as grace.

"Do not judge and you will not be judged; do not condemn, and you will not be condemned. Forgive, and you will be forgiven." *(Luke 6:37)*

SOME QUESTIONS TO CONSIDER

1. Can you think of someone whom you completely misjudged at first?
2. Do you suppose Aunt Sarah is completely unaware of the mischievous character of her cats?
3. Would we be better off if we could remember only the good things about the past, and forgot about all the bad things?
4. If you were Tramp, how would you explain your past to Lady?
5. Would you like to be a criminal court judge, pronouncing sentences on other people?
6. What is your favorite Christmas memory?

CHAPTER 15:
BATTLING DRAGONS:
SLEEPING BEAUTY

A great portent appeared in heaven: a woman clothed with the sun, with the moon under her feet, and on her head a crown of twelve stars. She was pregnant and was crying out in birth pangs, in the agony of giving birth. Then another portent appeared in heaven: a great red dragon, with seven heads and ten horns, and seven diadems on his heads. His tail swept down a third of the stars of heaven and threw them to the earth. Then the dragon stood before the woman who was about to bear a child, so that he might devour her child as soon as it was born. And she gave birth to a son, a male child, who is to rule all the nations with a rod of iron. But her child was snatched away and taken to God and to his throne; and the woman fled into the wilderness, where she has a place prepared by God, so that there she can be nourished for one thousand two hundred sixty days.

And war broke out in heaven; Michael and his angels fought against the dragon. The dragon and his angels fought back, but they were defeated, and there was no longer any place for them in heaven. The great dragon was thrown down, that ancient serpent, who is called the Devil and Satan, the deceiver of the whole world—he was thrown down to the earth, and his angels were thrown down with him.

Then I heard a loud voice in heaven, proclaiming.

Now have come the salvation and the power

and the kingdom of our God
and the authority of his Messiah,
for the accuser of our comrades has been thrown down,
who accuse them day and night before our God.
But they have conquered him by the blood of the Lamb
and by the word of their testimony,
for they did not cling to life even in the face of death.
Rejoice then, you heavens
and those who dwell in them!
But woe to the earth and the sea,
for the devil has come down to you
with great wrath,
because he knows that his time is short!"

So when the dragon saw that he had been thrown down to the earth, he pursued the woman who had given birth to the male child. But the woman was given the two wings of the great eagle, so that she could fly from the serpent into the wilderness, to her place where she is nourished for a time, and times, and half a time. Then from his mouth the serpent poured water like a river after the woman, to sweep her away with the flood. But the earth came to the help of the woman; it opened its mouth and swallowed the river that the dragon had poured from his mouth. Then the dragon was angry with the woman, and went off to make war on the rest of her children, those who keep the commandments of God and hold the testimony of Jesus.

Revelation 12:1-17

When it was first released in January 1959, Walt Disney's *Sleeping Beauty* claimed the title for being the most expensive animated feature ever made—costing $6 million. It remains perhaps the most technically elaborate film in the Disney animated library—originally produced in wide-screen Technirama with a stereophonic sound track.

Based on the classic fairy tale, the story begins with the birth of the princess Aurora, named after the dawn by her parents, King Stefan and his Queen. A gala party of celebration is held in the castle. Among the guests are another monarch, King Hubert, and his young son, Prince Phillip. Together the kings announce that one day their children will be married.

Also attending the party are three good fairies—Flora, Fauna, and Merryweather. Each of them comes to bestow a gift on the newborn child. Flora presents the gift of beauty. Fauna presents the gift of a song.

But then, just as Merryweather is about to bestow her gift, the serenity of the scene is shattered by a shocking interruption. It is the arrival of the wicked fairy known as Maleficent, who materializes out of the flames of a supernatural fire. Maleficent expresses her displeasure at having not been invited to the party. She proceeds to invoke a curse upon the newborn child:

"I, too, shall bestow a gift on the child. Listen well, all of you. The Princess shall indeed grow in grace and beauty, beloved by all who know her. But, before the sun sets on her sixteenth birthday, she shall prick her finger on the spindle of a spinning-wheel and die."

When the King orders his guards to seize Maleficent, she dissolves once again into those supernatural flames and disappears. Thus evil has cast a pall on a glorious celebration.

Come back now nineteen centuries from the present to a time in human history when another force of evil has cast a pall on a celebration. The Christian Church is in its infancy, just decades following the triumph of Easter. The message of the gospel is being joyfully embraced and shared across social and cultural barriers that have long divided the human race—Jew and Greek, rich and poor, slave and free, young and old, male and female.

However, this equalitarianism has caught the attention of the Caesars—the succession of Roman emperors—who know instinctively that their power is undermined by everything the Church represents. In a tyrannical empire where Caesar claims to be a god, it has become treason to claim that Jesus Christ is Lord. So Christians are facing imprisonment, even martyrdom, for their faith.

John, the author of the book of Revelation, is one of them. He is a prisoner on the island of Patmos. His book is a prophetic vision that John wants to share with his fellow Christians. Although his words may sound cryptic to you and me, John's use of apocalyptic language and symbols could be readily understood by most of those who first received his message.

In John's vision, the ultimate supernatural shape of evil is represented by a dragon—"that ancient serpent, who is called the Devil and Satan, the deceiver of the whole world" *(Revelation 12:9).* This dragon once sought to devour a woman's newborn child. The woman, in John's vision, is the community of God's people—the messianic community. The child is the Messiah—Christ himself—"who is to rule all the nations with a rod of iron" *(Revelation 12:5).*

But, lo and behold, at birth "her child was snatched away and taken to God and to his throne" *(Revelation 12:5).* In John's vision, the birth of the Messiah was not the Nativity but the Cross. It was Christ's faithfulness unto death that took him to the throne of God.

The result was that "war broke out in heaven" *(Revelation 12:7).* The consequence was that all the powers of evil have been defeated and banished forever from God's heavenly realm. "The great dragon... was thrown down to the earth, and his angels were thrown down with him" *(Revelation 12:9).* The only place now left for evil to exercise its treachery is on earth.

Now, although John had a particular message for his own contemporaries—fortifying their faith for the onslaught of persecution at the hands of Roman imperialism—John's message remains timeless. He is speaking to you and me. And the first thing John is telling us is that we need to take seriously the reality of evil in the world. It rages around us like the malevolence of an angry dragon.

The noted historian, Arnold Toynbee, repeatedly found himself wrestling with questions such as why a nation as literate as Germany could come under the spell of a monster like Adolph Hitler. He finally concluded that what we call "civilization" is little more than a thin crust of custom covering a molten mass of evil always in danger of boiling up and causing terrible destructiveness.

Evil—as the prophet John describes the dragon *(Revelation 12:3)*—has many heads, many faces, many disguises, many allies. Its appearance may be as vicious as a dictator's brutality or as subtle as a moment's rationalization. It may be embodied in entire social systems or in a single person's compromise.

Therefore the first arena for any of us to beware of its presence is in the recesses of our own heart. When we're honest with ourselves, we have to admit that evil is both dreadful and fascinating to us. One little boy said to another, "Listen carefully when you mom tells you not to do things. It give you all kinds of neat ideas."

There's something in even the youngest heart that flirts with what is wrong as well as what is right. It's almost predictable. A little girl was looking through a book entitled *Child Psychology, Ages Five Through Ten* that her mother was reading. Turning to one of her friends, the girl said, "Wow, you should read what a stinker I'm gonna be next year!"

Thomas Jefferson was a person who always wanted to believe in the innate goodness of human beings. One of the accomplishments in which he took greatest satisfaction was the establishment of the University of Virginia. It opened its doors in March of 1825 with forty students and several distinguished faculty members from Europe.

Because of Jefferson's belief in the innate goodness of human nature, there were hardly any rules and regulations concerning student discipline. It was a bold experiment in confidence. How did the students respond to this confidence? They walked out of classes. They gambled in the dormitories. They frequented the local taverns and got roaring drunk. They threw stink bombs into the rooms of the faculty. One night they marched around the campus howling, "Down with the European professors!" They even threw bricks when some of the faculty members tried to restore order.

The following day there was an emergency meeting of the Board of Visitors, the governing body of the University. Thomas Jefferson was the first to speak. He stood up and declared that the incident had been one of the most painful in his life. He tried to continue speaking but found he was too overcome with emotion. He sank down in his chair with tears in his eyes. The Board went on to draft a strict code of rules and regulations that would henceforth govern campus behavior.

Like Thomas Jefferson, we'd like to believe in the innate goodness of human beings, yet we keep being confronted by the reality of evil. Sometimes it appears overwhelming. When cruel tyrants consolidate their position by murder and brutality, when twisted emotions lead to savage behavior, when power and affluence turn a deaf ear to the cries of human misery.....that's when we're painfully aware of the presence of evil in the world.....even as those early Christians saw it prowling the earth like a bloodthirsty dragon, exercising its power in the cruel barbarism of ancient Rome.

In the story of *Sleeping Beauty*, it is Maleficent who personifies evil. She has poisoned the joyous occasion of the princess Aurora's birth with the pronouncement of her bitter curse.

After she is gone, the third good fairy, Merryweather, proceeds to present her gift. Explaining that she doesn't have the power to cancel Maleficent's spell, she can at least modify it. The prick of the spinning-wheel on Aurora's sixteenth birthday will bring sleep instead of death. As in the story of *Snow White and The Seven Dwarfs*, only the kiss of true love will be able to end the sleep.

Although King Stefan orders that all spinning wheels in the kingdom be destroyed, Flora, Fauna, and Merryweather realize that this offers little protection from the evil of Maleficient. They determine that, with her parents' permission, they will disguise themselves as three peasant women, and take the princess into the forest and raise her there. To maintain the secret, they will voluntarily forego the use of their magical powers until Aurora's sixteenth birthday.

Thus the years pass, until the critical day finally arrives. Maleficent is in her domain, the Forbidden Mountains, brood ing in anger that her cohorts, a demonic army of Goons, have failed to discover the location of the princess. When they tell her they have examined every cradle in the land, she explodes at their stupidity for still looking for a baby. She turns to her peccant pet, a raven, and orders it to search for Aurora.

Aurora is now a lovely young maiden. The good fairies are planning a surprise sixteenth birthday party for her. They send the princess out to pick berries, so that they can make a new dress and bake a birthday cake. Aurora—now called Briar Rose, as part of her protection—strolls through the woods and begins singing with the animals, who gather around her. She tells them of a prince she has met "once upon a dream".

It so happens that Prince Phillip is riding on his horse nearby. He hears her singing and is enchanted by her voice. Following a mishap involving Phillip being dumped in a puddle, the two meet. Although they were betrothed by their parents sixteen years ago when Aurora was born, they have no idea of each other's name or true identity. When they part, they promise to meet again that evening at the cottage.

Meanwhile the three good fairies have become frustrated by their inability to create an acceptable dress and a presentable cake. Merryweather persuades the others to break the moratorium on the use of magic, so as not to spoil the birthday celebration. In the subsequent exchange of magical powers, a disagreement emerges between Fauna and Merryweather over the color of the dress. The residue from their pink and blue blasts of magic emerges from the cottage and catches the eye of Maleficent's raven.

When Aurora returns, she is delighted with her surprises. She tells her protectors that it is the happiest day of her life. She has met, and fallen in love with, a stranger. With poignancy, they reveal to her her true identity and tell her that she is already betrothed to a Prince. She breaks down in tears.

At King Stefan's castle, the two royal fathers are discussing wedding plans when Prince Phillip arrives and announces, to their dismay, that he has found the girl he intends to marry. He then leaves for their intended rendezvous at the cottage.

The three good fairies bring Aurora to the castle to be reintroduced as royalty. But they leave her alone for a moment so that she can compose herself. In that moment, Maleficent, whose raven has tracked down the princess, hypnotizes the girl and lures her to an upper chamber, where the touch of a spinning wheel's spindle plunges her into a deep sleep.

When the good fairies discover the scene, they decide to cast a merciful spell of sleep upon all the people at the castle, to spare them the knowledge of what has happened. In the process they hear Prince Phillip's father use the phrase, "once upon a dream". They suddenly realize that the stranger with whom Aurora is in love and the Prince to whom she is betrothed are one and the same. They hurry off to the cottage, where the young couple planned to meet.

Once there, they discover that Phillip has been abducted by Maleficent's Goons and carried off to her stronghold in the Forbidden Mountains. They make their own journey there and discover that the Prince is being held captive by chains in the dungeon. They use their magic to cut the chains. And to do battle with Maleficent and her evil army, they give him two implements: the Shield of Virtue and the Sword of Truth.

Here, once again, our story of fantasy suggests a <u>second</u> fundamental reality: <u>We are not defenseless against the power of evil</u>.

In the book of Revelation, John declares to his fellow Christians that they, too, have a shield of virtue: which is to "keep the commandments of God" *(Revelation 12:17)*, to remain faithful even unto death. They, too, have a sword of truth: which is to "hold the testimony of Jesus" *(Revelation 12:17)*, to declare allegiance to him above all others, including Caesar.

However ferocious and powerful evil may appear, it can always be battled with virtue and truth.

The son of Mahatma Gandhi was asked what he remembered best about his father. It was not the political power of his leadership in India's quest for freedom that the son mentioned. It was his father's commitment to speak the truth. As an example, whenever Gandhi was to make a public statement, he would always first send a copy to his opponents asking for the correction of any errors. The result was that his speeches were so truthful as to be totally disconcerting to his enemies.

Ghandi was eventually assassinated for his truthfulness. Jesus was crucified for his truth. And as John predicted in the book of Revelation, many early Christians were put to death for declaring their allegiance to Christ in a Roman court.

Bertrand Russell, the noted British philosopher, was once asked whether he would be willing to die for his beliefs. "Of course not," he replied, "after all, I may be wrong." Doesn't he speak for many of us whose other loyalties sometimes prove stronger than our loyalty to virtue and truth?

There's an old story about a law firm that was interviewing candidates for a new position at the firm. Each candidate was asked a deceptively simple question: "Tell us, what does two plus two make?" The first candidate replied straightforwardly: "Two plus two make four." The second candidate was a little more roundabout: "Well, there are several possibilities. Two and two make four, but so do three and one—or two and one-half plus one and one-half—they also make four. So, it's all a matter of choosing the right approach." When the third candidate was asked the question, he became quiet. He looked around furtively, then he asked if he could close the door for privacy. Then he came over close, leaned toward the interviewers, and said, "Tell me, what would you like it to make?"

When we begin to compromise virtue and truth, we forfeit the very shield and sword that are our armor against the power of evil.

Today our own confrontations with evil may not carry the same threat of martyrdom that Rome lashed out against the early Church. Yet significant and poignant sacrifices continue to remain the cost of a commitment to virtue and truth.

In Henrik Ibsen's play, *An Enemy of the People*, Dr. Thomas Stockmann is the medical supervisor of the mineral baths in a resort town. These baths are the livelihood of the community. But several visitors have become ill after bathing in them. His investigation reveals that the waters have been contaminated by refuse from tanneries above the town. He reports his findings to the town's authorities, but they fear financial disaster if the report is not suppressed. The doctor's brother Peter is the mayor. Peter tells him to retract his findings, to write a false report. But the doctor refuses to do so. The mayor says he will fire him if he doesn't cooperate. When the doctor discusses the issue with his wife, she urges him to think of his family and retract his findings. She knows that if he doesn't, they will lose their income. At this point their two young sons come into the room. Looking at them, he is convinced that he must risk everything to be a person of virtue and truth. He says he wants to be able to look his boys in the face when they grow up. And his integrity costs him dearly. He comes to be regarded as "an enemy of the people".

There is a price attached to virtue and truth. It may involve sacrifices in friendship, prestige, health and career. For many of those early Christians it involved the sacrifice on earth of life itself. Sometimes the whole world can seem to be swallowed up in evil, and to stand up for virtue and truth is both lonely and dangerous. And yet, in the poetic words of James Russell Lowell:

"Though the cause of evil prosper, yet 'tis truth alone is strong. Truth forever on the scaffold, wrong forever on the throne. Yet that scaffold sways the future, and, behind the dim unknown, standeth God within the shadow keeping watch above his own."

Returning to the story of *Sleeping Beauty*, the shield of virtue and sword of truth have been entrusted to the character of Prince Phillip, who must do battle with Maleficent's infernal legion of Goons in order to escape the dungeon and the fortress. With his shield and sword, and help from Flora, Fauna, and Merriweather, the Prince is reunited with his horse. Together they race toward the castle where everyone has fallen asleep.

When Maleficent discovers his heroic mission, she casts

yet another evil spell—causing the castle to be swallowed up in a forest of thorns—declaring:

> "A forest of thorns shall be his tomb,
> Borne through the skies on a fog of doom.
> Now go with a curse and serve me well:
> Round Stefan's castle cast my spell!"

But with his shield and sword, the Prince is able to hack his way through the thorns toward the castle entrance. In utter rage, Maleficent now pulls out all the stops. She hurls herself in front of the Prince and transforms herself into an enormous fire-breathing dragon. The ultimate showdown has commenced.

It's a breathtaking battle. A young Prince would seem to have little chance against a supernatural force of evil as terrifying as a dragon. But the Prince is not daunted. His shield protects him from the flames the dragon aims at his body. And just when everything seems lost—with the Prince prone on his back atop a precarious precipice and the dragon towering over him for the kill—he hurls the sword at the dragon's heart.

It finds its mark, and the dragon tumbles to its death. This force of evil has been defeated. Prince Phillip hurries to the sleeping Aurora. His kiss not only restores her, but breaks the spell and awakens everyone in the castle. A great and wonderful celebration unites them all.

So, too, does a great and wonderful celebration provide the culmination of the prophet John's vision in the book of Revelation. Here is the <u>third</u> and final, truth which John conveys as a promise: In the eternal warfare between goodness and evil—between God and all his adversaries—<u>the final victory has already been assured</u>.

John sees beyond every present tribulation to an eternal

triumph. With his closing words, he describes "a new heaven and a new earth" *(Revelation 21:1)* where evil has been conquered forever and "death will be no more" *(Revelation 21:4)*.

Throughout his vision John holds before his friends in the early Church the example of Jesus, whose crucifixion was only a prelude to his Easter triumph. He is assuring them that, even if they have to die for their faith, God will use their very death to plunge the sword of truth into the heart of evil—the dragon and its allies such as imperial Rome. Ultimately, evil is doomed. Ultimately, faithfulness is redeemed.

John's vision of virtue and truth gaining their ultimate victory over evil provided a banner of confidence and courage for the early Church. Many did indeed go to their deaths. But their faithfulness was the very instrument God used to inspire others and to ultimately achieve victory.

As the great historian Will Durant observed in his classic work *Caesar and Christ*: "There is no greater drama in human record than the sight of a few Christians—scorned and oppressed by a succession of emperors, bearing all trials with a fierce tenacity, multiplying quietly, building order while their enemies generated chaos, fighting the sword with the word, brutality with hope, and at last defeating the strongest state that history has known. Caesar and Christ met in the arena, and Christ had won!" [15]

The cruelty of ancient Roman imperialism may have disappeared, but not our own earthly battle with evil. Evil keeps finding other manifestations, other allies. Like a dragon, it still bares its teeth and spits its fire and thrashes its tail. It remains the enemy of every sacrifice for integrity and every impulse of unselfishness and every outpouring of love.

But evil can still be battled with the shield of virtue and the sword of truth. For evil's power is only mortal. The provisions of the gospel are immortal. They are the gifts and resources by which God animates eternity and promises to embrace you and me forever.

SOME QUESTIONS TO CONSIDER

1. What dragons—forces of evil—are most menacing in our society today?
2. Should King Stefan and his Queen have invited Maleficent to the celebration of Aurora's birth, in order to avoid her displeasure?
3. Does human history seem to be making any progress against its dragons, the forces of evil?
4. Should the three good fairies have told Briar Rose/Aurora all along that she was really a princess?
5. Does faith in Christ protect us from the forces of evil?
6. If you could be personally present at any moment in the story of *Sleeping Beauty*, when would it be?

CHAPTER 16:

ONE HUNDRED AND ONE BLESSINGS: *ONE HUNDRED AND ONE DALMATIANS*

When Jesus saw the crowds, he went up the mountain; and after he sat down, his disciples came to him. Then he began to speak, and taught them, saying:

"Blessed are the poor in spirit, for theirs is the kingdom of heaven.
Blessed are those who mourn, for they will be comforted.
Blessed are the meek, for they will inherit the earth."

Matthew 5:1-5

One Hundred and One Dalmatians was the first Disney animated feature to be set in a contemporary time frame. Based on a story by Dodie Smith, the opening scene zeroes in on a London bachelor apartment to identify the voice of the narrator. It turns out to be a Dalmatian named Pongo. He verbally introduces us to his human companion, a struggling song-writer named Roger Radcliff, whom Pongo calls his "pet".

It is Springtime, and Pongo observes that the bachelor life is not everything it's cracked up to be. In fact, it's downright dull. He decides that female company would be good for both Roger and himself. So he looks out the window, hoping to spot suitable candidates in the neighborhood. After assessing a number of ladies walking their dogs, he sees a beautiful female Dalmatian, accompanied by an attractive human companion. Pongo concludes they would make a perfect match for himself and Roger. But, as he watches, the females are disappearing in the direction of the park. Pongo knows he must compel Roger immediately to go for a walk. Unfortunately, it's not yet five o'clock—the traditional time for that activity. So Pongo uses his nose to advance the clock. Roger notices the time, picks up his hat and pipe, and takes the hint that Pongo has engineered.

Once outside, Pongo strains at his leash to pull Roger in the direction of the park. After much jockeying on Pongo's part, the determined Dalmatian discovers the females resting at a park bench. He leads Roger to the spot, but Roger is content to pass by, settle down on a bank of the lake, and smoke his pipe. What can Pongo do? He decides to snatch Roger's hat and deposit it on the bench beside the young woman. However, by the time Roger gets there, the females have gotten up to leave. So Pongo pulls Roger after him, eventually circling both humans, so that they are entangled in his leash. In their effort to extricate themselves, the humans lose their balance and fall into the water together.

Instead of a romantic encounter, Pongo seems to have caused a disaster. As the two thoroughly drenched humans pick themselves up, the young woman reaches into her purse for a handkerchief to dry her face. But it is thoroughly soaked. Humbly, Roger reaches into his own back pocket and offers her his own handkerchief. But, of course, it also is wringing wet. So there are the two of them, utterly humbled, still standing in the lake. As the young woman looks at Roger, holding before her this dripping hanky, she cannot help but begin to laugh. Roger, too, perceives the humor in the situation and shares her laughter.

The next scene is a church where Roger and the young

woman, whose name is Anita, are promising to live together as husband and wife. Within hearing distance in the courtyard are Pongo and the female Dalmatian, named Perdita. Their paws are linked. And we know they, too, have made a commitment to one another.

We next see the two couples about six months later. They are living in a modest apartment. They are as happy as they can be—in spite of their meager circumstances—because they have each other. And, on top of that, Pongo and Perdita are expecting a litter of puppies soon. What could make life any more blessed than that?

Long ago Jesus described the truly blessed in life. The collection of his ethical teachings commonly referred to as "The Sermon On The Mount" *(Matthew 5-7)* begins with a set of declarations called the "Beatitudes". They are Jesus's descriptions of those who are blessed with the highest promises of happiness.

Human beings have forever been obsessed with happiness and how to achieve it. The pursuit of happiness fuels our society's most lucrative industries. Books, businesses, products of all kinds promise us what we want most in life: true happiness. Merchants of every description offer us their answers. Skin-tight jeans on a well-toned figure—that is true happiness! Investment security for our retirement years—that is true happiness! Effusive friends drooling over our home furnishings—that is true happiness! Glamorous members of the opposite gender eager to be close to us because of our mouthwash—that is true happiness! (One little boy, however, saw a television commercial depicting a considerable amount of smooching and hurried to his father with an unusual request: "Dad, I think I want bad breath.")

Yet the yearning for true happiness often proves, ironically, to be the source of much unhappiness. The restless search for happiness uproots many a prodigal, warps many a friendship, strains many a family, dissolves many a home. Someone says to himself, "I'm not really happy with this. Maybe that will make me happy instead." A mud of dirt and tears cakes the feet where many a leap has been made toward imagined happiness.

That's what make the "Beatitudes" of Jesus so profound. True happiness, he says, is not something to be boasted about, or bought, or bargained for. It's a blessing. It's the joy of discovering that life's highest gifts may not mirror society's passionate priorities. Jesus turns the world's ideas of happiness upside down. In doing so, he seeks to turn the world's upside-down value system rightside up.

He declares, first of all, "Blessed are the poor in spirit, for theirs is the kingdom of heaven" *(Matthew 5:3)*. What a shocking reversal of our assumptions! Everything in the fabric of our society seems to teach that happiness is the consequence of being wealthy—rich in things and rich in spirit. To be flush in your bank account, to be assertive in your personality, to have the world at your feet—these are the goals by which people seek contentment.

But Jesus reverses that logic and shifts its focus. The deepest happiness—the happiness that is imperishable—comes not from our belongings, he says, but from our belonging. It springs from the blessed sense of humility that acknowledges our dependency upon one another, upon the rest of creation, upon our Creator. We belong to a higher source of life than ourselves alone. To the degree that we are "poor in spirit"—humble in our outlook and relationships, whatever our social standing—to that same degree we are open to the joy of being blessed by higher dimensions of happiness than we could ever engineer for ourselves.

A woman in a suburban community donated many hours each week to volunteer service in a local hospital. It gave her great satisfaction and happiness to contribute, in humble ways, to the well-being of the patients who were coping with the problems that required their hospitalization. One day she was engaged in a particularly dirty task when another woman said to her, "My dear, I wouldn't do that for a thousand dollars." She looked up, smiled and replied, "Neither would I."

Centuries ago a prosperous citizen of Florence, the Gonfalonier Pier Soderini, was a patron of the artist Michelangelo. After Michelangelo had completed his magnificent statue of David, Soderini came to inspect it. With a haughty gesture he pointed at the sculpture and complained that the nose was all out of proportion to the rest of the figure. He insisted it had to be corrected. Instead of protesting, Michelangelo climbed up the scaffold with his hammer and made a few loud blows on the marble that changed nothing. Each time he would let fall some marble dust that he had concealed in his hand. When he climbed down, his pretentious critic declared, "Now you have given it life indeed!" With his wealth and pride, Soderini could have been described as "rich in spirit". But with his humility and talent, we know that Michelangelo was truly blessed.

So. too, as the story of *One Hundred and One Dalmatians* unfolds, the human characters, Roger and Anita, as well as the Dalmatians, Pongo and Perdita, are blessed with a happiness that springs, not from vanity and prosperity, but from the humble pleasures they enjoy in their relationship with one another.

"Blessed are the poor in spirit, for theirs is the kingdom of heaven."

However, a threat to the happiness in that home enters the scene one day with a visit from one of Anita's schoolmates—the outrageous Cruella DeVil. Cruella is the epitome of a person who is "rich in spirit"—proud of her possessions and arrogant in her desires. Among other things, she declares that she "lives for furs". She enjoys wearing the coats of beautiful and exotic animals. Having learned that the Dalmatians are expecting a litter of puppies, she has determined she must have them for herself. When she is told that the puppies have not yet been born, she hastily exits the house.

Roger, who has just composed a catchy tune expresses his distrust of Cruella in the lyrics: "The world was such a wholesome place until Cruella, Cruella DeVil." Sensing that Cruella wants her puppies, Perdita has hidden herself under a stove. Pongo finds her and tries to comfort her. She tells him how happy she was at first. But now she wishes they weren't going to have any puppies after all.

Nevertheless, on a stormy night. the puppies are born. The household Nanny reports to Roger and Pongo the number of the offspring, which keeps getting revised: Eight, Ten, Eleven, Thirteen, Fourteen, Fifteen. Then, sadly, she appears with a little bundle. "Fourteen," she says. "Just fourteen. We lost one." As they mourn this apparent loss, Roger holds the little bundle and begins to rub it. And before long it responds. The fifteenth puppy is alive after all!

Just as they all rejoice in this happy turn of events, who should appear at the door but Cruella! She wants to see the puppies. When she discovers they have no spots, she calls them mongrels. But when she learns that they will acquire their spots after a few weeks, she insists on buying them all. "Name your price!" she demands. When Roger tells her they are not for sale at any price, she stomps out of the house in a fury, vowing that she will "get even".

Several weeks later, while the Radcliffs and the adult dogs are out for an evening walk, a pair of shady crooks named Jasper and Horace force their way into the house and steal all fifteen puppies. As it turns out, they have been hired by Cruella DeVil to commit this crime. The Radcliff home, which had been filled with such happiness, suddenly becomes a place of mourning.

One of the most seemingly quixotic things Jesus ever said is expressed in the second of his "Beatitudes": "Blessed are those who mourn, for they will be comforted." *(Matthew 5:4)*

How startling! If there's anything we don't want to do, it's to mourn, to grieve, to suffer the heartbreak that is the emblem of compassion. Yet again Jesus challenges our conventional assumptions. We cannot hope to understand blessedness, he says, without feeling sorrow. Happiness and sorrow—blessedness and mourning—are as intimately related as flesh and blood or life and death. To the degree that we isolate ourselves from the experience of mourning, we shut ourselves off from the avenues to joy.

Ancient Stoic philosophers such as Epictetus were afraid of sorrow and taught the suppression of emotion: "Love your wife and your children, but not so much that you will be hurt when they die." Jesus would shake his head at such advice. How much happiness could there be in such a love?

Handel used the words of Isaiah to describe the *Messiah* in music as "a man of sorrows and acquainted with grief." Our highest concept of God is that of a Lord who cares—who embraces human pain with tears in his eyes. Never does God stand aloof from a broken heart. God seeks to make his presence known. And God's presence is the gift of comfort and hope.

Jesus would have us expand and deepen our sympathies, for we thereby enlarge the relationships that fill life with meaning and joy.

Albert Schweitzer left the accolades of a great European career because there was mourning in the African jungle. To a place where suffering and illness were epidemic, he came with healing and comfort. A little girl in the mission school, not understanding the uses of anesthesia, wrote these words in her diary: "Since the Doctor came here, we have seen the most wonderful things happen. First of all, he kills the sick people; then he cures them, and after that he wakes them up again." Norman Cousins was one of Schweitzer's greatest admirers. Following a visit, he declared that to be in Schweitzer's presence was like "a new revelation of happiness."

"Blessed are those who mourn, for they will be comforted."

The mourning in the Radcliff home is the evidence of love in the Radcliff home. The Dalmatian puppies have been kidnapped. When the efforts of Scotland Yard prove fruitless, Pongo determines to employ the "Twilight Bark," a network of canine communication, in order to locate the puppies. Thanks to the barking of dogs of every description, the effort is successful. Word comes that the fifteen puppies—along with eighty-four other young Dalmatians bought from pet stores—are being held captive by Jasper and Horace in an old long-deserted country mansion owned by Cruella DeVil.

Pongo and Perdita begin the long and difficult trek to the mansion. Meantime, three animals who reported the location of the puppies—a cat named Sergeant Tibbs, a horse named the Captain, and a somewhat befuddled old sheepdog named the Colonel—observe Cruella's arrival at the mansion. Sergeant Tibbs, the cat, overhears Cruella as she orders Jasper and Horace to kill the puppies immediately for their coats. She had originally planned to raise the animals to maturity for their furs. But now the police search has triggered her impatience. She slams the door as she leaves.

Moments before Jasper and Horace can carry out their dastardly deed, Tibbs is able to marshal the puppies into exiting the room through a hole in the wall. When Jasper and Horace turn their attention to carrying out their grisly instructions, they discover that the puppies are no longer in the room.

A frantic chase begins inside the mansion. Just when the crooks seem to have the puppies trapped in the corner of another room, Pongo and Perdita burst through the window. They are able to divert Jasper and Horace while Tibbs leads the puppies outside. The adult Dalmatians then run from the house.

There is a grand reunion of puppies and parents in a barn down the road. When Pongo and Perdita discover there are 84 other puppies, in addition to their own, they determine they will bring them all back home to London. But soon an old truck approaches the barn. Jasper and Horace have been following the dogs' tracks. The Dalmatians succeed in leaving the barn just before the crooks enter it. Two well-aimed kicks by the horse named Captain deliver a unexpected surprise for the crooks. When they attempt to follow the tracks again, they cannot find them. The Dalmatians have begun walking on the ice, so that they will leave no tracks.

Soon Cruella herself joins the chase. Adding to the dogs' misery, a bitterly cold snow storm now threatens them. In the nick of time, a Collie leads them to the shelter of a dairy barn, where compassionate cows offer the puppies warm milk. All of them are grateful for the opportunity to rest. When the storm is over, the Collie directs them toward the village of Dinsford where a Labrador will meet them with more food. But this time Cruella spots their tracks and concludes that Dinsford is their destination.

When the Labrador meets the Dalmatians, he shares the good news that a van currently being repaired will soon be leaving for London, They can hop aboard for a ride home. But before they can get into the van, the three villains—Cruella, Jasper and Horace—arrive and begin prowling the street.

Pongo gets an idea. If they all roll in fireplace ashes, they will become so dark that they will no longer look like Dalmatians, but more like Labradors. This seems to work, as the dogs begin loading into the van right under the noses of their pursuers.

But then some drops of water melting from snow on a roof reveal their true identity, and the chase resumes. The van driver, unaware of the presence of the Dalmatians in the back of the van, is mystified and irritated when Cruella in her car tries to force him off the road. Subsequent roadway encounters undermine the villains, with the truck of Jasper and Horace crashing into the car of Cruella. The last we see of the treacherous trio is the sight of Cruella fuming at her henchmen in an off-road pile of rubble and snow.

Meanwhile, at home, Roger and Anita have been mourning the loss, not only of the puppies, but of Pongo and Perdita as well. They don't yet know the reason for the adult Dalmatians' disappearance. The fact that Roger's song about Cruella DeVil has become a hit recording offers little solace for their grief. But then the sound of dogs barking announces the arrival of all 101 Dalmatians. Sadness turns into gladness. The story ends blessedly with Roger resolving to move them all to the countryside, where they will establish a Dalmatian Plantation and live happily thereafter.

Long ago Jesus made a third observation about happiness: "Blessed are the meek, for they will inherit the earth." *(Matthew 5:5)*

Once again he confounds our contemporary assumptions. Doesn't meekness imply a cowardly wimp—someone who is frightened by his own shadow? And don't such people inherit nothing but ulcers and ridicule? Here's the difficulty of centuries of semantics. When the Bible talks about meekness, it's not a synonym for timidity. The mightiest figure in the Old Testament, Moses, is called the "meekest of men" *(Numbers 12:03—King James Version).*

Perhaps the best synonyms for our understanding would

be the words "gentle" and "disciplined". Jesus is saying that true happiness isn't the reward of impulsive aggressiveness. Impulsive aggressiveness is what starts children fighting, keeps adults quarreling, and sends nations to war. The earth cannot ultimately be inherited by belligerence, any more than the kingdom of God can be secured by tanks and bombers. Happiness is the fruit of gentleness and discipline, the patience in spirit that is considerate and controlled.

In the story of *One Hundred and One Dalmations,* ninety-nine puppies ultimately inherit their deliverance, not because of a brash display of force, but because a disciplined network of animals cared about them, located them, stood by them, and led them home. Meekness is not weakness. The most blessed victories on earth are those that are forged through cooperation and persistence. Instead of exercising brute intimidation, they embody a quiet commitment to compassion.

A wealthy man lost his wife when his son was just an infant. Into their home came a housekeeper to take care of the child. She embodied the qualities Jesus described as meekness. Gently and patiently for many years she cared for the boy. Then, tragically, the boy died in his adolescence. The man himself died, heart-broken, soon after the death of his son.

There were no other relatives, and no will was discovered. All that could be found were the man's handwritten instructions that the state should hold a sale to dispose of the personal effects at the mansion where the man had lived. The faithful housekeeper came to the sale, but not to buy any of the expensive items. She didn't care about furniture or silverware. There was a picture of the boy on the wall of his room. She had come to love the boy as if he were her own son. She wanted that picture by which to always remember him.

No one else was interested in the picture, so she paid very little money for it. When she brought it home, she decided to clean it, because it had been hanging on the wall for some time. As she took the glass out to wash it, she discovered some papers behind the picture. As she examined them, she discovered that it was the missing will. It declared that the man wished to leave his entire inheritance to the person who loved his son enough to cherish that picture.

"Blessed are the meek, for they will inherit the earth."

So it is that God has given the world God's Son. As we come to know him and love him, we discover a promise of joy that often confounds the world's ideas of happiness. We learn what it truly means to be blessed. And those blessings are beyond counting.....one hundred and one and more! For the grace of God is inexhaustible and eternal.

"Blessed are the poor in spirit, for theirs is the kingdom of heaven."

"Blessed are those who mourn, for they will be comforted."

"Blessed are the meek, for they will inherit the earth." *(Matthew 5:3-5)*

SOME QUESTIONS TO CONSIDER

1. When are you the happiest?
2. If you had fallen into the water, like Roger and Anita, would you have been amused or angry?
3. Why did Jesus say that those who mourn are blessed?
4. Do you suppose Cruella DeVil ever mourned?
5. Can you think of someone who is truly meek, in the sense of being gentle and disciplined?
6. If you were to play a character in *One Hundred and One Dalmations*, which one would it be?

CHAPTER 17:
A SWORD AND A STONE:
THE SWORD IN THE STONE

And David came to Saul, and entered his service. Saul loved him greatly, and he became his armor-bearer. Saul sent to Jesse, saying, "Let David remain in my service, for he has found favor in my sight." And whenever the evil spirit from God came upon Saul, David took the lyre and played it with his hand, and Saul would be relieved and feel better, and the evil spirit would depart from him.

Now the Philistines gathered their armies for battle; they were gathered at Socoh, which belongs to Judah, and encamped between Socoh and Azekah, in Ephes-dammim. Saul and the Israelites gathered and encamped in the valley of Elah, and formed ranks against the Philistines. The Philistines stood on the mountain on the one side, and Israel stood on the mountain on the other side, with a valley between them. And there came out from the camp of the Philistines a champion named Goliath, of Gath, whose height was six cubits and a span. He had a helmet of bronze on his head, and he was armed with a coat of mail; the weight of the coat was five thousand shekels of bronze. He had greaves of bronze on his legs and a javelin of bronze slung between his shoulders. The shaft of his spear was like a weaver's beam, and his spear's head weighed six hundred shekels of iron; and his shield-bearer went before him. He stood and shouted to the ranks of Israel, "Why have you come out to draw up for battle? Am I not a Philistine, and are you not servants of Saul? Choose a man for yourselves, and let him come down to me. If he is able to fight with me and kill me, then we will be your servants; but if I prevail against him and kill him, then you shall be our servants and serve us." And the Philistine said, "Today I defy the ranks of Israel! Give me a man, that we may fight together." When Saul and all Israel heard these words of the Philistine, they were dismayed and greatly afraid.

1 Samuel 16:21-17:11

Saul clothed David with his armor; he put a bronze helmet on his head and clothed him with a coat of mail. David strapped Saul's sword over the armor, and he tried in vain to walk, for he was not used to them. Then David said to Saul, "I cannot walk with these; for I am not used to them." So David removed them. Then he took his staff in his hand, and chose five smooth stones from the wadi, and put them in his shepherd's bag, in the pouch; his sling was in his hand, and he drew near to the Philistine.

The Philistine came on and drew near to David, with his shield-bearer in front of him. When the Philistine looked and saw David, he disdained him, for he was only a youth, ruddy and handsome in appearance. The Philistine said to David, "Am I a dog, that you come to me with sticks?" And the Philistine cursed David by his gods. The Philistine said to David, "Come to me, and I will give your flesh to the birds of the air and to the wild animals of the field." But David said to the Philistine, "You come to me with sword and spear and javelin; but I come to you in the name of the Lord of hosts, the God of the armies of Israel, whom you have defied. This very day the Lord will deliver you into my hand, and I will strike you down and cut off your head; and I will give the dead bodies of the Philistine army this very day to the birds of the air and to the wild animals of the earth, so that all the earth may know that there is a God is Israel, and that all this assembly may know that the Lord does not save by sword and spear; for the battle is the Lord's and he will give you into our hand."

When the Philistine drew nearer to meet David, David ran

quickly toward the battle line to meet the Philistine. David put his hand in his bag, took out a stone, slung it, and struck the Philistine on his forehead; the stone sank into his forehead, and he fell face down on the ground.

So David prevailed over the Philistine with a sling and a stone, striking down the Philistine and killing him; there was no sword in David's hand.

1 Samuel 17:38-50

Walt Disney's *The Sword in the Stone* is an adaptation of T. H. White's story about the boy who would become King Arthur. The title refers to a legend, central to both the book and the film, that the next king of England will be the one who has the power to remove a sword that has been embedded in a large stone.

The story begins during a dark time in the kingdom. Conflict and chaos have prevailed since the last good King died. No consensus can be reached as to the rightful heir to the throne. Lawlessness prevails. People live in fear of one another. The strong prey upon the weak. The only glimmer of hope has been the miraculous appearance in London of a sword buried in a stone and anvil. On it an inscription reads: "Whoso pulleth out this sword of this stone and anvil is rightwise king born of England." But, alas, not even the strongest knight is able to extract the sword. So the darkness continues, and the sword in the stone is all but forgotten.

The first characters we meet live deep in the woods. They are Merlin the Magician, who sports a long, white beard, and his pet, a slightly irascible owl named Archimedes. With his wizard's clairvoyance, Merlin tells Archimedes that they will soon be entertaining a guest—a scrawny boy about eleven or twelve years old. It is Merlin's intention to take the boy under his tutelage. Together they have an important destiny to fulfill.

Sure enough, as predicted, a boy literally drops through the roof. He has ventured into the woods to retrieve an arrow belonging to his foster brother, Kay, who is much older and brawnier than himself. Spotting the arrow atop a tree, the boy climbs the branches, only to lose his balance and tumble into Merlin's front room. The boy tells the wizard that his name is Arthur, but everyone calls him Wart. Merlin explains his determination to provide Wart an education, to help him become the person he is intended to be.

Merlin and Archimedes then accompany Wart back to the castle where the boy lives as a virtual servant of his adoptive guardian, Sir Ector, Kay's father. When they arrive, Wart is scolded for his absence and sent to the kitchen to work an extra four hours. Merlin is not immediately made welcome. But after a chilling demonstration of his magical powers, he is reluctantly offered residence in the delapidated northwest tower of the castle. The tower provides scant shelter, however, as Merlin discovers that evening when a rainstorm reveals a multiplicity of leaks.

A lone traveler arrives in the midst of the storm. It is Sir Pelinore, a friend of Sir Ector. He brings news from London. A great Tournament will be held on New Year's Day. And the winner will become the next King. Excited by the prospect, Sir Ector tells his son Kay that he must begin training intensively for the tournament, so that he can become a knight and conquer all the other contenders for the throne. Sir Ector goes on to promise Wart that if he sticks to his duties, he may act as Kay's squire—his armor-bearer.

There's a story of another young armor-bearer recorded in the seventeenth chapter of the Old Testament book of First Samuel. The boy's name is David. He is in the service of Saul, who is near the end of his reign as King of Israel. David, too, lives in a dark time of conflict and struggle for power. The Israelites are at war with the Philistines.

Three of David's older brothers are soldiers in the Israelite army. David himself not only serves as an armor-bearer for King Saul, but he also tends his father's sheep in Bethlehem. So his duties take him back and forth from army encampment to home, just as a crucial face-off develops between the Philistine army and the Israelites on a battleground west of Bethlehem.

The tension mounts when an enormous Philistine warrior appears—a champion known as Goliath, of Gath. He is described as being incredibly huge and strong. He is about nine and a half feet tall. He wears bronze armor and carries a large iron spear. He issues a challenge: Let the Israelites choose one of their number to fight with him. If that person can defeat Goliath, the Philistines will become slaves of the Israelites. But if Goliath triumphs, the Israelites must serve the Philistines. "Today I defy the ranks of Israel!" taunts this giant combatant, "Give me a man, that we may fight together." *(1 Samuel 17:10)*

Soon thereafter David returns from home to the scene of battle, bringing food for his brothers and others. And he hears Goliath repeat his challenge. As he looks around him, he sees that all the soldiers are frightened. None will accept the challenge. So David seeks out King Saul and offers himself.

The struggle for power—so evident in ancient Israel, as well as in England during the Dark Ages of *The Sword in the Stone*—continues to preoccupy the world today. The renowned psychoanalyst, Alfred Adler, concluded, from a lifetime of observation, that the primary motivating force in human life is the will and the need for power. However, a perennial question remains. What is real power? Where does power truly and ultimately reside?

<u>One</u> kind of power is <u>the power of brawn</u>, the power of brute force. This is the power represented by Goliath in the

Old Testament, as well as the impending competition of the Royal Tournament in *The Sword in the Stone.* The Tournament promises to award the crown to the mightiest in muscle, the conqueror in combat, the one who can dominate others by the sheer intimidation of his own strength. This is the kind of power that thrives on, and leads to, weakness in others.

Some of us encountered such power at an early age—perhaps in the form of a neighborhood bully. A nine-year-old boy came home from school one day with a bloody nose, a black eye, and torn clothing. It was obvious he had been in a fight and had lost. While his father was patching him up, he asked his son what had happened. "Well, Dad," replied the boy, "I challenged Billy to a duel, and I made the mistake of giving him his choice of weapons. I never thought he'd choose his sister."

Others encounter this kind of power at an early age in the form of domineering parents. Children do indeed want their parents to be strong. It's a parent's role to assume a certain power of authority over a child. But that power is meant to be exercised in a way that the child, initially weak, can become stronger herself. Something is terribly wrong if parental authority turns into parental dominance.....if a parent's need to prevail comes at the expense of causing a child to habitually fail. Power in a home ought to be a common commitment rather than a competitive contest.

To that end, many ministers such as myself have eliminated from our wedding ceremonies that phrase with which a wife promises to "obey" her husband. Few contemporary marriages embrace the notion that strength in a relationship involves one person's servile obedience to another. In fact, when one minister asked the bride, "Do you promise to obey?" she answered, "Do you think I'm crazy?" Unfortunately, the flustered groom jumped the gun and said, "I do!"

Domination acts to perpetuates weakness—whether it be

a person living with a domineering spouse, or a child living with a tyrannical parent, or an employee working for an abusive boss, or a social group struggling against discrimination. There is something demonically wrong about the kind of power that depends upon the exploitation or perpetuation of someone else's weakness and fear.

This kind of power is the power represented by Goliath.....the kind of power that dominated the ancient world with brute force. A nation proved its strength by conquering and preying upon weaker nations. A ruler proved his power over his people by keeping them subservient to the monuments of his own glory. There remains wholesale evidence of this kind of power around the world today—wherever human rights are crushed and human dignity degraded under the shadow of those whose power depends upon domination, whose strength thrives on weakness, who stand like the spectre of Goliath on the contemporary horizon.

So, returning to the story of *The Sword in the Stone,* young Arthur, called Wart, lives in a castle and a kingdom where might made for right, and power seemed to belong to those whose strength came from preying upon the weakness of others.

But Merlin the Magician has assumed responsibility for the education of Wart. And while Wart's foster brother Kay practices jousting for the New Year's Tournament, Merlin attempts to teach the boy that brains are more important than brawn. To help him learn this, Merlin uses his magic to transform them into a pair of small fish in the castle moat. As they swim together, he explains the predatory facts of nature with a song: "In human life it's also true, the strong will try to conquer you. And that is what you must expect unless you use your intellect. Brains and brawn, weak and strong, that's what makes the world go round."

The song is interrupted by the attack of an enormous and voracious pike, who tries to devour Wart in his form as a small fish. Wart uses his brains—first to temporarily trap the pike's jaws in a link of the drawbridge chain. When the pike breaks free and opens its mouth to devour Wart, Wart manuevers a stick into the mouth to keep it wedged open. Finally, with some unexpected help from the owl Archimedes, Wart escapes the pike and becomes human again.

His next adventure comes when Merlin turns them into squirrels. He wants Wart to empathize with one of nature's tiniest creatures with the most enormous problems. However, the lesson is complicated by the appearance of two female squirrels. They become enamored of Wart and Merlin in their current form. Finally Merlin has to change himself and Wart back into humans. This breaks the heart of the squirrel who has become attached to Wart. She retreats into the hollow of a tree trunk in tears. Merlin points out to Wart, "You know, lad, that love business is a powerful thing. I'd say it's the greatest force on earth."

Wart's next incarnation is to become a little bird. But almost immediately he is pursued by a fierce hawk. The chase ends with Wart tumbling down the chimney of a forest cottage belonging to the Mad Madam Mim. Mim is a practitioner of black magic and a rival of Merlin. She tries to destroy Wart, but Merlin arrives just in the nick of time to save him. Mim then challenges Merlin to a wizards' duel, with the two of them changing themselves into various animals. Mim transforms herself into several large and ferocious beasts—ultimately a fire-breathing dragon. Merlin, on the other hand, employs his intellect to outwit her. He finally becomes a microscopic germ that conquers the dragon by infecting it with a disease. Once again, Wart learns the lesson that brains can be more important than brawn.

In the Old Testament, the boy David demonstrates the

same lesson in his battle with the giant, Goliath. Having volunteered to accept the challenge, David discovers that he cannot wear the usual soldier's armor. The sword, the helmet, the coat of mail—they are all too bulky and unfamiliar to him. He discards them and takes only his shepherd's staff and sling and bag, into which he puts five smooth stones *(1 Samuel 17:40)*. He will rely on his mind more than his muscles.

And here is a second kind of power in the world today—the power of brains, the power of reason. This is the power represented by David in the Old Testament, the kind of power Merlin seeks to instill in young Arthur.

A woman once attended a meeting sponsored by the League of Women Voters. She sat silently through a two-hour discussion of issues involving international trade. When it was over, she thanked the speakers and said, "I'm glad I came, because I was so terribly confused about international trade. Of course, I'm still confused, but now on a much higher plane."

Most of us wish we had more brain power to help us climb on top of our confusions. We're embarrassed when we don't comprehend what others seem to know. Sometimes we resort to defense mechanisms, hoping that no one else will know that we don't know. We may laugh at jokes we don't understand or nod in agreement to erudite statements we can't fathom. We'd like people to think we have an exceptional mind, but secretly we wish it were far more exceptional. We admire those whose brains have forged great accomplishments, solved great problems, invented great things. We dream of what we could do if we only had a little more brain power.

Early in his automotive career Henry Ford granted a subcontract for certain engine parts. But he specified that these parts had to be delivered in wooden boxes of a precise size. The boxes themselves had to be secured with screws instead of nails. He even pinpointed the location and size of the screws. The subcontractors accepted the conditions because they wanted the business. But among themselves they agreed that Ford had to be a lightheaded eccentric. Even some of Ford's own employees privately questioned his rationality. Then came the day the shipping boxes arrived. Henry Ford's eccentricity proved to be the product of his brain. The sides of the shipping boxes were exactly the size required of the floorboards for his automobiles. Even the screw holes were correctly sized and spaced. All that was needed was to slip them into place.

Whole industries, inventions, institutions may come into being because someone uses her brain. Someone figures out what to do and how to do it. Certainly when it comes to conducting a business, or governing a country, we'd like to think that the crucial decisions are being made by those in power using their brains. It's been said that God made us with two ends: one on which to sit, the other with which to think. Our success—perhaps our very survival—depends upon which end we use the most. Heads we win, tails we lose!

There's a perceptive scene in George Kaufman's play, *The President's Daughter.* A young man is standing in front of a portrait of his grandfather, who had been President of the United States. He announces aloud, "I think I can fill his shoes." His sister hears him and perceptively replies, "It's the other end of grandfather which was most important."

History itself teaches the lesson that, in the long run, brains are far more powerful than brawn. Whether it's an Aesop fable or an Uncle Remus story or a modern diplomatic crisis, the moral is the same: a show of intelligence is a show of force.

So, in *The Sword and the Stone,* Merlin asks young Arthur, called Wart, what he learned from observing the wizards' duel. Wart replies, "Knowledge and wisdom (are) the real power."

The time comes for the Tournament in London. Wart's foster brother Kay has honed his skills and muscles for the contest. He has become a knight, and Wart is acting as his squire. Surely the brawniest contestant will claim the title of King. The jousting has concluded, and the sword fighting is about to begin. But Wart suddenly discovers that he has forgotten to bring Kay's sword. He left it at the inn. In the company of Archimedes the owl, Wart rushes back to the inn, but no one is there to open the locked door.

Just when all seems lost, Archimedes points out a sword in the nearby church yard. But this sword is embedded in an anvil and stone. Knowing that it is his duty to provide Kay with a sword, Wart is determined to pull the sword from the stone. When he touches it, the sword is surrounded by the mysterious power of a heavenly light. Archimedes warns him to back away. But Wart persists and pulls the sword out of the stone.

When he arrives with it back at the Tournament, Kay begins to protest that it's not his sword. But then his father, Sir Ector, reads the inscription and realizes it is the miraculous "sword in the stone". The Tournament is halted while everyone goes to the church yard to review the evidence. When the sword is replaced in the anvil and stone, not even the strongest knights struggling together can remove it. But young Arthur again performs the miracle. It is at that moment when all those present know that he is destined to be their King.

Likewise, in the Old Testament story of David and Goliath, a miracle takes place. The boy David, armed only with his brains and his sling and five smooth stones, confronts the brawniest champion of the Philistines, who brandishes a spear and a javelin and a sword. But David brings to the challenge one more dimension of power. As he declares to Goliath: "I come to you in the name of the Lord of hosts, the God of the armies of Israel, whom you have defied. This very day the Lord will deliver you into my hand" *(1 Samuel 17:45-46).* In contrast to Goliath, who seeks only to squelch an enemy, David seeks to serve his God.

What happened on that battlefield outside Bethlehem has become one of the most often repeated stories of the human family. The boy with the stone slew the warrior with the sword. A wisely, carefully slung blow to the forehead of Goliath brought the giant to the ground. And the victory belonged to the honor of God.

The boy David would soon thereafter become the King of Israel, indeed perhaps the greatest King the nation would ever have. And like the legend of King Arthur in *The Sword and the Stone,* there was a power at work that was even greater than the confrontation between human brains and human brawn. There was a destiny unfolding, behind which was a power that is divine.

Here is a <u>third</u> kind of power available to you and me today—<u>the power of God's purposes and promises</u>. In the daily challenges of life our brains are likely to serve us better than our brawn. But the most crucial question is, Whom do we serve? Do we employ our brains and our brawn only in the service of our own selfish ambitions, or do we link our destiny to the purposes and promises that come from God?

It may never be our fate to become a King or a Queen. We may remain a knave instead of a knight. But the drama of God's kingdom continues to unfold. And each of us has a unique role to play in that drama. God is a creative artist who fashions eternity out of every expression of faith and hope and love. A squire may become a statesman. A shepherd may become a savior. An enemy may become a friend. What was once a battlefield may become a sanctuary of peace.

Many years ago the Northern Baptist Convention—now

the American Baptist Convention—had convened a meeting in the midwest. Among those present was a group of Native American Indian Christians, who were sitting together near the front of the assembly hall. A missionary who worked among the Native Americans—his name was Tyson—began to speak. Addressing the Indians, he said: "I was once your enemy. I was in Custer's campaign in Wyoming, and I fought you to the death."

As Mr. Tyson went on to describe one of the battles, an aged Native American chief slowly rose to his feet. He raised his hand and was recognized by the presiding officer. "Mr. President," he said with great deliberation, "I was in that battle. We fought like demons to stop the palefaces." There was a hush that gripped the souls of everyone present. The old chief continued: "I was Mr. Tyson's bitter enemy. But now I have heard him preach the gospel. And I know we are brothers."

The presiding officer made an invitation: "Will you come forward and shake hands with your old-time enemy who is now your Christian brother?" Somewhat awkwardly the old chief made his way to the aisle of the assembly hall, then took slow, measured steps toward the platform. As the two men came closer to one another, tears began to well up in their eyes. Without saying a word, without even shaking hands, they put their arms around each other in a reconciling embrace. And the entire congregation rose spontaneously to sing a beloved hymn:

"Blest be the tie that binds our hearts in Christian love.
The fellowship of kindred minds is like to that above."

When our brawn fails us—even when our own brain fails us—God alone will never fail us. And surely the redemptive energy of God's purposes and promises is the greatest power of all!

SOME QUESTIONS TO CONSIDER

1. Would you rather be a lot stronger or a lot smarter than you are right now?
2. Do you believe people have clairvoyant powers, like Merlin, and can see the future?
3. Who is the most intelligent person you know?
4. If, like Wart/Arthur, you could become any animal for a while, what animal would it be?
5. What promise from God means the most to you?
6. If you became King, like Arthur, what would be your first decree?

CHAPTER 18:

FRIENDS AND ENEMIES IN THE JUNGLE OF LIFE: *THE JUNGLE BOOK*

Then Pharaoh commanded all his people, "Every boy that is born to the Hebrews you shall throw into the Nile, but you shall let every girl live."

Now a man from the house of Levite went and married a Levite woman. The woman conceived and bore a son; and when she saw that he was a fine baby, she hid him three months. When she could hide him no longer she got a papyrus basket for him, and plastered it with bitumen and pitch; she put the child in it and placed it among the reeds on the bank of the river. His sister stood at a distance, to see what would happen to him.

The daughter of Pharaoh came down to bathe at the river, while her attendants walked beside the river. She saw the basket among the reeds and sent her maid to bring it. When she opened it, she saw the child. He was crying, and she took pity on him, "This must be one of the Hebrews' children," she said. Then his sister said to Pharaoh's daughter, "Shall I go and get you a nurse from the Hebrew women to nurse the child for you?" Pharaoh's daughter said to her, "Yes." So the girl went and called the child's mother. Pharaoh's daughter said to her, "Take this child and nurse it for me, and I will give you your wages." So the woman took the child and nursed it. When the child grew up, she brought him to Pharaoh's daughter, and she took him as her son. She

named him Moses, "because," she said, "I drew him out of the water."
Exodus 1:22-2:10

The last animated feature with which Walt Disney was personally involved before his death was the studio's freewheeling adaptation of Rudyard Kipling's collection of stories, *The Jungle Book.* Since its initial release, it has remained among the most popular Disney films with both the critics and the public alike.

The story begins in the jungles of India where a panther named Bagheera hears an unusual sound. When he investigates, he discovers a baby boy—a "mancub," as he calls him. The baby is lying in a basket on a broken boat that has washed up on the river's bank. Knowing that the baby needs nurturing, Bagheera takes him to a family of wolves. A litter of cubs has just been born, and the human baby is immediately welcome among them. He is given the name Mowgli.

Several years pass. Mowgli is now a young lad. But word comes to the wolf pack that Shere Khan the tiger has returned to the vicinity. Shere Khan hates anything human, which means that Mowgli is in mortal danger. The council of wolves decides that Mowgli must leave, and Bagheera steps forward to offer to take him to the human settlement, the "man-village", where he will be safe.

In the Old Testament book of Exodus there's a story of another baby who is discovered in a basket along a river. He will be given the name Moses, because—as his adoptive mother declares—"I drew him out of the water" *(Exodus 2:10).* He had been put in the basket by his natural mother, because he, too, had an enemy. He was a Hebrew baby boy, and Pharaoh—the king of Egypt—was jealous and afraid of the Hebrews, the Israelites.

According to Genesis, the Israelites had come to Egypt during the generation of Joseph. They had been welcomed by the Egyptians, and Joseph had been a favorite in the king's court. As Joseph's generation died, the Israelites continued to multiply, "so that the land was filled with them" *(Exodus 1:7)*.

But a new king had brought a different and hostile attitude into Egypt. Assessing their numbers and their strength, he had begun to fear the Israelites. He imagined that, in the event of war, they might become allies of Egypt's enemies. So he had looked upon the Israelites themselves as enemies and made them slaves.

Furthermore, Pharaoh—the king—had ordered the Hebrew midwives to destroy all newborn male Hebrew children. However, fearing and honoring their God, they had not cooperated with Pharaoh. So Pharaoh had commanded, "Every boy that is born to the Hebrews you shall throw into the Nile" *(Exodus 1:22)*. Moses's mother, three months after giving birth to him, had put him a basket "among the reeds on the bank of the river" *(Exodus 2:3)*. Thus, through no fault of his own, Moses, like Mowgli, had a mortal foe from the moment he was born.

And here's <u>one</u> of the observations we must make about the jungle of life: Regardless of how innocent we are, regardless of how virtuous we are, regardless of how many friends we have, <u>we're going to have enemies as well as friends</u>. This may simply be the consequence of the predatory factor in the natural order of things, making the lion the natural enemy of the lamb, and the mouse the prey of the cat. Or we may create enemies because of our own behavior or lifestyle or value system. Or we may simply be the innocent target of someone else's jealousy, bigotry, or greed.

Whatever the reason, the Bible itself takes for granted the fact that we will have enemies. The Old Testament psalmist cried out, "O Lord, how many are my foes! Many are rising against me!" *(Psalm 3:1)*. And in the New Testament, Jesus uses the word "when," not "if"" as he says: "Blessed are you *when* people revile you and persecute you and utter all kinds of evil against you..." *(Matthew 6: 4).* He takes for granted the fact that anyone alive and breathing is going to have opponents, even as he himself had enemies who hounded him to the Cross.

An elderly man, on the occasion of his one hundredth birthday, was interviewed by a reporter. "A hundred years old," said the old gentleman, "and I haven't an enemy in the world." The reporter congratulated him on this observation. "Yep," continued the old fellow, "I've finally outlived them all."

Unfortunately it's virtually impossible for anyone to really outlive all his enemies. Whatever our age, there always seem to be a few around.

Indeed, there's a sense in which our enemies serve to define us. Their opposition to us bears witness to who we are. Whatever we represent, whatever nature and values and goals are bound up in our being, we're going to find forces lined up on the opposite side of those issues. Simply because he was a human being, Mowgli had an enemy in Shere Khan the tiger, who hated human beings. Simply because he was a Hebrew baby boy, Moses had an enemy in Pharaoh, who sought to destroy Hebrew baby boys.

Whoever you and I may be, whatever you and I may represent, we are bound to have enemies, known or unknown to us, who will seek to undermine us and our efforts, however openly or subtly. They may attack us with tooth and claw, bullets and bombs, name-calling and gossip.

The great nineteenth century English social reformer, William Wilberforce, was once asked by a flippant evangelist, "Brother, have you found peace?" And this tireless and courageous leader in the struggle against slavery and child labor in the British commonwealth replied simply: "No, my friend, I have found war."

To stand for anything—even justice and truth—always encounters a measure of opposition. There are enemies on the other side of every issue. Indeed, the more visibly we represent an idea or a cause, the more vigorous may be the antagonism we provoke. There's something in the fabric of human existence that guarantees that, whoever we are, whatever we represent, we will have enemies.

So it is, in *The Jungle Book,* that Bagheera knows even better than Mowgli how dangerous an enemy Shere Khan is. That is why he seeks to take Mowgli to the safety of the man-village. But Mowgli resists. He doesn't want to leave the jungle. He doesn't take seriously the threat represented by the tiger. Raised as a wolf, Mowgli is convinced that he can take care of himself.

But that night, as the two of them sleep on a branch high up in a tree, Mowgli is spotted by a large python name Kaa, another natural enemy. Kaa succeeds in hypnotizing Mowgli and is about to swallow him when Bagheera wakes up and comes to the rescue.

The two of them next encounter a herd of elephants—a jungle patrol—being drilled in military fashion by their leader, Colonel Hathi. Mowgli attempts to join the parade, as if he were a little elephant. But when Colonel Hathi discovers that this new recruit is a human boy, he loses his temper. Bagheera intervenes and assures the elephant that he is taking Mowgli back to the man-village.

As they start off again, Mowgli rebels. He insists that he will not go with Bagheera. When Bagheera tries to pull him loose from a tree, the panther slips, falls into the river and cracks his head on a log. Disgusted with Mowgli's stubbornness, Bagheera walks away, leaving the boy alone in the jungle.

Along comes the happy-go-lucky bear named Baloo. An affection between the boy and the bear quickly develops, and

Baloo begins teaching Mowgli how to be a bear. When Baloo demonstrates a bear growl, Bagheera hears it from a distance. He rushes back to the scene, feeling guilty now that he left Mowgli to himself. But when he sees that Mowgli is in the company of Baloo, he rolls his eyes and calls the bear a "shiftless, stupid jungle bum". Mowgli, in the meantime, has decided he does indeed want to be a bear.

Mowgli's next adventure is to be kidnapped by a group of monkeys, who take him to their leader, a portly orangutan named King Louie. King Louie insists that Mowgli teach him how to create fire. This, the orangutan is convinced, will allow him to become a human being. He expresses his desire in a song: "I Wanna Be Like You." But Mowgli is helpless to comply with this request. Bagheera and Baloo finally extract him from this predicament.

That evening, while Mowgli sleeps, Bagheera convinces Baloo that the boy will remain in mortal danger unless he is taken to the man-village. Baloo promises to break the news to Mowgli. But when he does, Mowgli feels like he is being betrayed. He runs away from his two closest jungle friends. Baloo and Bagheera try to enlist the elephant patrol to search for Mowgli. Unfortunately, Shere Khan overhears the conversation and becomes aware of Mowgli 's existence and his nearabouts.

Having broken away from Bagheera and Baloo, Mowgli has another encounter with Kaa the python. Kaa craftily tries to convince the boy that he is truly his friend. He sings a song: "Trust in me. Just in me. Shut your eyes, and trust in me. You can sleep safe and sound knowing I am around." But all the while, Kaa is wrapping his coils around the boy, preparing to eat him.

And here is a <u>second</u> observation we might make: In the jungle of life, <u>we may mistake our enemies as friends and our friends as enemies.</u> Appearances and impulses can be deceiving. An enemy like Kaa the python may pose as a friend, so as to take Mowgli off guard in order to devour him for dinner. Human history and human relationships are checkered with numerous stories of "Trojan Horses," enemies who disguise themselves as friends.

On the other hand, we may sometimes mistake as enemies those who truly are our friends.

Mowgli falsely perceives Bagheera and Baloo as his enemies. He desperately wants to stay in the jungle, the only home he has ever known. But they know all too well the danger that threatens him in the form of Shere Khan. In reality, in wanting to take Mowgli to the man-village, they are seeking only what is best for Mowgli. They are offering him wise and loving counsel. But Mowgli thinks they are against him.

Likewise, I can imagine a young boy named Moses many centuries ago grappling with the same confusion. Who is his enemy? Who is his friend? Having been left as a baby in a basket on the river by his Hebrew mother, he was discovered by none other than the daughter of Pharaoh himself, the king who was his bitter enemy. Pharaoh's daughter had come to the river to bathe. When she found him, she realized at once he must be a Hebrew child. But instead of harming him, "she took him as her son" *(Exodus 2:10)*.

Think of the conflict that must have existed in the mind of Moses—the natural son of a Hebrew woman, the adopted son of the Egyptian Pharaoh's daughter. Only when he becomes a young man does he become fully aware of how the Egyptians are oppressing the Hebrews. Indeed, one day when he observes an Egyptian beating a Hebrew, he proceeds to kill the Egyptian. *(Exodus 2:12)* Yet, not long after that, a fellow Hebrew asks Moses, "Do you mean to kill me as you killed the Egyptian?" *(Exodus 2:14)* And to futher complicate matters, Pharaoh himself hears about the incident, and seeks to kill Moses. So Moses is forced to flee to the land of Midian, no doubt confused about where his allegiance truly belongs.

We're not always clear about who are our enemies and who are really our friends. An unusual incident is reported to have occurred at the outbreak of World War I. The War Ministry in London dispatched a coded message to one of the British outposts in the inaccessible areas of Africa. The message read: "War declared. Arrest all enemy aliens in your district." The War Ministry soon received this reply: "Have arrested ten Germans, six Belgians, four Frenchmen, two Italians, three Austrians, and an American. Please advise immediately who is the enemy."

That's a question we keep asking. And we can never be certain we know the final answer. Sometimes our enemy of the moment is our friend in the end, and the thing that clouds our perspective may be our own enmity. You remember that little girl who kicked up such a terrible fuss one evening that she was required by her family to eat dinner by herself at a separate table in the corner. Her grace for that meal was directly out of the Old Testament. "O Lord," she prayed with a pout, "I thank thee for preparing a table before me in the presence of my enemies."

A child facing parental discipline may temporarily be tempted to think of the parent as an enemy. But, in most cases, it is the love of the parent for the child that is the true motive for the discipline. Likewise, demanding teachers, law-enforcement officers, corporate supervisors, are not always the enemy simply because they hold before us higher standards than our past performance. Occasionally those we view as enemies are in reality friends who ultimately have our best interests at heart.

A woman was driving home on the freeway late one night. Suddenly a big-rig truck pulled alongside her. The driver gestured for her to pull over. She knew nothing was wrong with her car mechanically. There was little traffic at that point on the freeway, and she began to dread the possibility of an assault. She pushed her foot lower on the accelerator, but the truck driver accelerated immediately behind her. She pulled off at the next exit, and the truck roared off the ramp after her. She was in a state of panic now. She screeched into an all-night gas station, jumped out of her car and rushed into the cashier's office. The truck barrelled into the station after her. But instead of running after her, the driver raced to the rear door of her car. He jerked it open and pulled out a man who had been hiding in the back seat—a man he had seen from the vantage point of his cab. The truck driver, whom the woman had feared as an enemy, saved her from a man who would otherwise have become her real assailant.

While never abandoning caution and good sense, you and I do well to remember that we may sometimes be mistaken about who are our enemies and who are our friends.

In *The Jungle Book,* after Mowgli escapes once again from the coils of Kaa the python, he finds himself in the company of four vultures. Now, if there are any creatures that a vulnerable child alone in the jungle might be tempted to regard as enemies, a quartet of vultures would seem to qualify. But, contrary to expectations, when they realize his predicament, they offer to make him one of their own, an "honorary vulture". They even sing him a song: "We're your friends to the bitter end."

Unfortunately the song is interrupted by the sudden appearance of Mowgli's fiercest enemy, Shere Khan himself. After counting to ten, the tiger leaps toward Mowgli to kill him. At that very moment Baloo appears and grabs the tiger by his tail. He's not able to stop Shere Khan. But he is able to slow him down sufficiently to allow the vultures to carry

Mowgli to safety.

Thwarted in his purpose, Shere Khan turns on Baloo and attacks him. Lightning strikes a tree and sets it on fire. The vultures tell Mowgli that fire is only thing that the tiger fears. So, while the vultures distract Shere Khan with dive-bombing manuvers, Mowgli ties a burning branch onto the tiger's tail. When Shere Khan becomes aware of the fire attached to him, he runs away in terror.

Attention now focusses on Baloo, who appears to have been killed by Shere Khan in their struggle. Bagheera the panther appears and assures Mowgli that Baloo will always be remembered. He eulogizes the bear's sacrifice, paraphrasing the words of Jesus: "Greater love hath no one than he who lays down his life for his friend." *(cf. John 15:13)* While Bagheera is speaking, Baloo, who is alive after all, regains consciousness and quietly enjoys the tribute being paid him. In fact, when Bagheera finishes, Baloo calls out for more, thereby exasperating his eulogizer.

Happily reunited, Baloo assures Mowgli that nothing will come between them again. Then they hear a voice singing nearby. It turns out to be that of a young girl. She's singing about her home, the man-village. She has come to the river to fill a jar with water. Mowgli is immediately curious. As he watches, he becomes enchanted by her. He senses an affinity with her. She is unlike anything Mowgli has ever seen before, yet—at the same time—she is like him. He moves closer to get a better look. The girl notices Mowgli, and she is equally enchanted. She pretends to drop the jar, and it rolls near Mowgli. She starts back toward the man-village, quietly inviting Mowgli with her eyes to follow her. Tentatively, but willingly, he retrieves the jar, fills it with water, and begins to follow her into the village.

At a distance, Baloo urges Mowgli to come back into the jungle. But Bagheera knows that the village is meant to be

Mowgli's home. And so when Mowgli looks back at his friends and shrugs his shoulders in a gesture of inevitability as he joins his new companion, Bagheera wisely announces: "Mowgli is where he belongs now." And Baloo, still insisting that Mowgli would have made a great bear, cannot help but agree.

In the Old Testament, the young Moses, too, faces the question of where, and to whom, he truly belongs. As his story unfolds, the answer to that question comes to Moses through an encounter with God. "In a flame of fire out of a bush" *(Exodus 3:2)*—God reveals himself as the God of his Hebrew ancestors—"the God of your father, the God of Abraham, the God of Isaac, and the God of Jacob." *(Exodus 3:6)* Moses learns that it is God's will that the Israelites be delivered from their bondage in Egypt to a new home—"a land flowing with milk and honey." *(Exodus 3:8)* And God has chosen Moses to be their leader.

Few stories in the Bible are as moving as the subsequent drama of Moses confronting Pharaoh, in the name, and with the power, of God.....finally leading his own people away from their oppression in Egypt into the wilderness. It is in the wilderness where they are given the Law—the Commandments—and blessed with a vision of their destiny, and finally given a home.

And here, in the third place, is the question life asks of every one of us: Where are we ultimately at home? To answer that question, we first have to ask ourselves the question Mowgli and Moses had to ask: Who are we? Raised as a wolf cub, taught by Baloo how to be a bear, inducted as an "honorary vulture," Mowgli ultimately had to come to terms with the fact that he was a human being and belonged in the man-village. Born as an Israelite, raised as an Egyptian, hated by Pharaoh, loved by Pharaoh's daughter, Moses ultimately had to come to terms with the fact that God had chosen him to lead his people out of Egypt.

Who are we? We usually identify ourselves with labels—a name, an address, an occupation, a social security number. We may identify ourselves with possessions—what we have, what we own, what we have accumulated. We may identify ourselves with associations. One little boy was bragging to another about his father's fraternal memberships: "My Dad's a Lion, a Moose, and an Elk!" His young friend was duly impressed. "Gee," he replied, "how much does it cost to see him?"

But there's a larger meaning to our existence than all our labels, possessions, associations. Who we really are eludes the measurement of an accountant or a chemist or a surgeon. Who we are is ultimately bound up in our relationship with God.

A young medical student once announced that he had dissected a human body and had found no soul. Therefore, he concluded, human beings have no souls. His wiser mentor replied, "That's interesting. When you dissected the human brain, did you find a thought? When you dissected the human eye, did you find vision? When you dissected the human heart, did you find love? Yet don't you believe in the existence of thoughts and vision and love? Just because you cannot locate the human soul on a medical chart doesn't mean it doesn't exist."

So it is for you and me. The greatest truth about us—call it our "soul"—is the reality of our relationship with God. Who we are depends upon *whose* we are. It is God who created us. It is God to whom we belong. We are God's children. We are God's family. To acknowledge and embrace our relationship with God is to discover the grace where we are now and forever at home.

Long ago the Old Testament prophet Isaiah offered a vision of the messianic kingdom: "The wolf shall live with the lamb, the leopard shall lie down with the kid, the calf and the lion and the fatling together, and a little child shall lead them. The cow and the bear shall graze, their young shall lie down together; and the lion shall eat straw like the ox. The nursing child shall play over the hole of the asp, and the weaned child shall put its hand on the adder's den." *(Isaiah 11:6-8)*

It is a vision of the jungle transformed into an eternal realm of peace and joy, where ancient enemies become harmonious friends and stubborn rivalries dissolve into faithful relationships. It is the vision, according to Isaiah, that will find expression with the coming of a Messiah.

The gospel is the "good news" that the Messiah has indeed come. In the person of Jesus Christ God has acted to reconcile all creation to himself. There is a path that leads out of the jungle into God's heart. The compass is grace. The first step is faith.

SOME QUESTIONS TO CONSIDER

1. Is the Middle Eastern saying true: "The enemy of my enemy is my friend"?
2. Do you think Mowgli and Shere Khan could ever be friends?
3. Can you remember a time when someone you thought was an enemy turned out to be a friend?
4. Is Bagheera justified in calling Baloo a "shiftless, stupid jungle bum"?
5. What three things are most important in making a home?
6. Because of his experience, do you think Mowgli would grow up to become a tiger hunter?

CHAPTER 19:
THE EYES OF MICKEY MOUSE

"No one after lighting a lamp puts it in a cellar, but on the lampstand so that those who enter may see the light. Your eye is the lamp of your body. If your eye is healthy, your whole body is full of light; but if it is not healthy, your body is full of darkness. Therefore consider whether the light in you is not darkness. If then your whole body is full of light, with no part of it in darkness, it will be as full of light as when a lamp gives you light with its rays."

Luke 11:33-36

Mickey Mouse was once described by New York's Metropolitan Museum of Art as the "greatest historical figure in the development of American art". A number of stories have circulated concerning his creation.

According to one story that Walt Disney himself liked to tell, he and his wife Lillian were traveling home by train from New York, where Disney had just lost the rights to his previous cartoon character, Oswald the Lucky Rabbit.

In Disney's own words: "Out of the trouble and confusion stood a mocking, merry little figure. Vague and indefinite at first. But it grew and grew and grew, and finally arrived: a mouse. A romping, rollicking little mouse. By the time my train had reached the Middle West, I had dressed my dream mouse in a pair of red velvet pants with two huge pearl buttons." [16]

Disney thought about naming this new character Mortimer, but his wife preferred the name Mickey. Other historians suggest that, although Walt's inspiration was the genesis for Mickey's personality, the world's most famous mouse largely owes the design of its physical appearance to the talents of the animator, Ub Iwerks.

The first Mickey Mouse cartoon to be released was *Steamboat Willie*, on November 18, 1928, and it featured a synchronized sound track. It was an immediate sensation. Soundtracks were added to two other already produced Mickey shorts, and they were also released. And Mickey Mouse began his ascent in popularity.

Now, it must be said of Mickey—as it could be said of every one of us—his appearance has changed over the years. Beginning as a rather scrawny and rubbery rodent, Mickey today has become a refined corporate symbol. His personality has mellowed from a sometimes mischievous menace to a more dignified and affable celebrity.

What I'd like to focus on are Mickey's eyes. As Frank Thomas and Ollie Johnston have pointed out in their classic treatise on animation, *The Illusion of Life*, Mickey's eyes have undergone an artistic metamorphosis over the years.[17] Perhaps that change is suggestive of an evolution that God intends to take place in your life and mine as well.

Among the teachings of Jesus is his declaration that "Your eye is the lamp of your body. If your eye is healthy, your whole body is full of light; but if it is not healthy, your body is full of darkness." *(Luke 11:34)* It's as he was saying there is something pivotal about the shape and state of our eyes.

Mickey's actual <u>first</u> incarnation was in a film entitled *Plane*

Crazy, one of those to which a sound track was subsequently added, following the success of *Steamboat Willie*. In this initial appearance, Mickey has wide, goggle-like eyes—almost as if they are expressing a perpetual sense of wonder at the dynamics of the world around him.

It is wonder about flight that animates this first story. Charles Lindburgh has just completed the historic nonstop solo flight from New York to Paris. Mickey is studying a picture of "Lindy" as the barnyard animals help him build a crude airplane. Finally it's ready. A dachshund is wound up into a coil in the fuselage of the plane to provide the power, and Mickey is off. Unfortunately, an immediate collision with a tree ends the flight, and Mickey begins to pout. Then suddenly his eyes light upon an old jalopy, which he converts into another plane, utilizing among other things, the tail of a passing turkey.

At this point Minnie Mouse makes her debut, bringing Mickey a lucky horseshoe. He invites her aboard and, with the help of that flexible dachshund, the pair is airborne. Unfortunately, Mickey is bounced out of the plane and begins to chase it, trying to reboard. The plane itself begins to chase a cow, who ends up hanging onto the tail section. Mickey grabs the cow's utters, only to be splashed with milk. When the cow falls off the plane, Mickey commandeers her at full gallop to jump back on. When Minnie pulls his ears in fright, the steering wheel comes off in Mickey's hands. The plane then begins wildly careening around the countryside until Mickey reconnects the steering wheel.

With the plane under control, Mickey begins to flirt with Minnie. He blinks those big goggle eyes at her. But she decides this is inappropriate behavior under the circumstances and gives him the cold shoulder. In a juvenile response, Mickey accelerates the plane, so that Minnie falls out. Then he maneuvers the plane to catch her again. This time he reaches over and gives her a kiss. Minnie is anything but pleased, and proceeds to jump out of the plane. Fortunately her bloomers act as a parachute to bring her safely to the ground. Mickey is less fortunate as he now completely loses control of the plane and crashes into another tree. On the ground, that lucky horseshoe lands on his head. Mickey tries to make light of the situation with Minnie. But she turns up her head and walks away. Mickey tosses the horseshoe away, but it boomerangs and comes back to ring him in the neck.

Plane Crazy, the earliest Mickey Mouse story, depicts a wide-eyed, curious, impulsive, uninhibited, wonder-filled character discovering the eccentricities of life, and the consequences of one's own behavior.....very much as each of us begins her own life with a healthy, child-like vision brimming with curiosity and wonder.

A baby-sitter once said to her young charge, "Isn't it wonderful how little chicks get out of their shells?" The child nodded, looked up at her with wide eyes, and replied: "What beats me is how they get in!"

We're surrounded by a wonder-filled world in a miraculous universe. Look up at the stars—millions of them making a single galaxy, and millions of galaxies comprising the universe and millions of those stars so immense that room could be found for millions of our own Sun in one of them.

Then look at a single drop of water—containing millions upon millions of molecules—you might even say galaxies of electrons. A little one-celled animal in that drop of water might be composed of more than a hundred billion atoms.

Then look at a human being, described by the physicist Sir Arthur Stanley Eddington as "almost precisely halfway in size between an atom and a star." Shakespeare's words are a dramatic understatement: "What a piece of work is a man!"

Consider the eye itself, and the wonderful process of converting light rays into color and sight. Consider an ear, and the curious vibrations of bones and nerves that communicate a Beethoven symphony. Consider the digestive system and how the body can convert food into energy. Consider the white corpuscles in the blood stream and how they can absorb and carry off infection. Above all, consider the brain and the intricate, incredible processes that allow us to think, to plan, to remember.

Our lives are nothing beyond prison sentences if they don't begin with a wide-eyed sense of curiosity and wonder. Woe to us if the routine of our days encrusts our outlook with boredom or cynicism.

I read somewhere that the chairman of the parent company of Wham-O, John Bowes, once sent a gift of several thousand Frisbees to an orphanage in Angola. He hoped that the children there would enjoy one of his company's most famous toys. A few months later a representative of the company happened to visit the orphanage. He was told that the children were thrilled with their gifts. What wonderful plates they were off of which to eat! And they could carry water so well. In fact, they even proved handy in catching fish. When the representative explained how Frisbees were actually intended to be used as a toy—as flying discs—the children could scarcely contain themselves with even greater delight over this exciting new possibility they hadn't yet imagined.

Would that we all could see life with such wide-eyed wonder and enthusiasm—much as that mouse named Mickey brought to the screen in the very first moments of his animated career.

But now, in the <u>second</u> place, let's look at Mickey's eyes a decade later in one of his greatest roles: as the *Brave Little Tailor*. Over the years Mickey's eyes had evolved from being erratically goggle-like to becoming <u>large, solid pupils</u> on his face—as if now they are more <u>focused on specific tasks and</u>

goals in each of his adventures.

In *Brave Little Tailor* Mickey is a humble clothier in a medieval kingdom threatened by a giant. We first see Mickey focused on patching a garment. A number of houseflies buzzing around his head begin to distract him. So he focuses his attention on eliminating the bothersome insects, which he swiftly accomplishes with a pair of fly swatters. Proud of his achievement, he throws open the window and announces to a group of citizens outside that he just killed seven with a single blow. What he doesn't realize is that they've been talking among themselves about the giant, and they assume he is, too. The misunderstood news about Mickey's prowess begins to spread, and finally reaches the king.

The king summons Mickey to his court and asks him if he really killed seven with one blow. Mickey proceeds to describe with great exaggeration his victory. Duly impressed, the king appoints him "Royal High Killer of the Giant". As the drastic misapprehension suddenly dawns on Mickey, he tries to decline the appointment. But the king's daughter, played by Minnie Mouse, persuades her father to offer her hand in marriage as a reward. She rushes over and covers Mickey's face with kisses and—with his eyes now focused on her—Mickey accepts the challenge.

So, amidst the cheers of the populace, Mickey leaves the protection of the city's gate to seek out the giant. It's not long before he encounters him—an oafish brute fifty times Mickey's size. Mickey tries to hide in a cart-load of pumpkins, but the giant sits down on a country house and proceeds to swallow the pumpkins and Mickey in a single gulp. He washes them down with a well-full of water. Mickey manages to use the dangling well bucket to escape, and he lands in a pile of hay covered by a tarp.

The giant picks up the hay, wrapping it in the tarp, and puts it in his mouth for a smoke. When he lights it with a stove from inside the house, Mickey begins to sneeze and pops out of the hay. Seeing Mickey, the giant tries to grab him. But Mickey is too quick and dashes up the giant's sleeve. When the giant reaches into his own sleeve to catch him, Mickey uses his tailor's scissors to cut himself out of the shoulder. Then he takes his needle and thread to imprison the giant's hand in the sleeve. Rappelling like a mountain climber, he encircles the giant with more thread, bringing him crashing to the ground.

The final scene shows a sleeping giant, imprisoned by Mickey's tailor threads, generating the power for a whole carnival with his snoring breath. And riding the carousel with Mickey is the princess Minnie, who had been the focus and inspiration for the *Brave Little Tailor's* triumph.

Mickey's eyes—solid pupils during these middle years of his career suggest the kind of transition from childhood wonder to adult concentration and focus that God intends for each of us to experience.

When Jesus talked about the eye being the lamp of the body, it was in reference to the light upon which the eye is focused. "Consider whether the light in you is not darkness." *(Luke 11:35)* In other words, Jesus is emphasizing the decisive nature of our life's orientation—specifically, that which is our primary focus.

As we begin to mature, life makes increasing demands upon us. We confront opportunities and responsibilities that call for choices and decisions. We have to choose between goals, careers, ideologies, ethics. We discover we can never get anywhere if we try to go in all directions at once.

The psychiatrist Victor Frankl has written: "Unless a person wishes to drown, he has to become selective..... Selectiveness means that we have to be responsible for what is important and what is not, what is essential and what is not, what is valuable and what is not, what is meaningful and what is not.

We have to be capable or become capable of such decision making."

A young man who was starting his freshman year at college—away from home for the first time—began unpacking his suitcases, which his mother had packed for him. In the process of putting all his clothes in the drawers, he discovered two long narrow strips of cloth amidst his pants and shirts and underwear. For quite a while it was a mystery what those two pieces of cloth were. But then as he studied the pattern, and recognized the design, it came to him. They were the strings of his mother's apron. She had cut them off for him. It was a wonderful lesson to remind him of his new level of self-determination and responsibility, and how important it was for him to focus on his education.

Irving Berlin lived to the age of 101. Born in Russia, immigrating to America when he was only four years old, he wrote more than a thousand songs. *God Bless America, White Christmas, Easter Parade:* these are just a few of his creations. As long as he was able, he was focused on making music. In his later years, he made the comment: "The question is, 'Are you going to be a crabby old man, or are you going to write another song?'"[19]

The mature life is the life that is focused—the life that chooses goals and works for them.....the life that acknowledges duties and remains faithful to them.....the life that embraces relationships and invests in them.

The eyes of Mickey Mouse have undergone other graphic expressions over the years. His solid pupils were often nicked or sliced in comic strips and other forms of art. But eventually his eyes evolved into the style and shape with which he is depicted today.....eyes very much like our own eyes, with <u>pupils centered in a field of white</u>—and eyelids that close and blink. They are eyes that have the <u>gift of perspective</u> to add to their wonder and their focus.

And Mickey's personality in these later years has demonstrated that perspective. He no longer always needs to occupy the spotlight as the wonder-struck young pilot or the focused little tailor. He is content to be a gentle neighbor and friend who is just as concerned about the welfare of others as he is about himself.

An example of this is the story of *Mickey's Christmas Carol*, which, in 1983, was the first theatrical Mickey Mouse cartoon to be released since 1953—thirty years earlier. Although he is credited as being the star, he is content to assume the supporting role of Bob Crachit in Disney's version of the famous Charles Dickens tale.

Scrooge McDuck, appropriately enough, plays the role of Scrooge in the story. We meet him as he arrives at his counting house. There his overworked, underpaid employee, played by Mickey—is putting a lump of coal into the stove. Scrooge angrily asks him what he is doing. Mickey explains he's trying to thaw out the ink. Scrooge grumbles that Mickey used a piece of coal last week and orders him to get to work. Mickey reminds him that tomorrow is Christmas and pleads for half a day off. Scrooge reluctantly agrees, but warns Mickey that it means he'll be docked half a day's pay.

Scrooge's nephew Fred arrives. He's played by Donald Duck. He wishes Scrooge a "Merry Christmas", presents him with a wreath, and invites him to come the following day for Christmas dinner. Scrooge's response is to wish his nephew a "Bah, Humbug!", to jam the wreath around his shoulders, and to kick him out the door. Soon a rat and a mole come through the door to ask Scrooge for a donation on behalf of the poor. Scrooge argues cynically that if he gives money for the poor, the poor won't be poor any more. No one will need to collect for them, and the rat and the mole will be out of a job. And he certainly wouldn't want to put anyone out of a job on Christmas Eve. Then they, too, are ushered out with a slam of the door.

That night Scrooge is visited by the ghost of his deceased partner Jacob Marley, played by Goofy. The ghost is doomed to wear chains for all eternity because of his greed and selfishness on earth. He warns Scrooge that an even worse fate awaits him unless he heeds the spirits who will visit him throughout that night.

Then the spirits come. One is the spirit of Christmas past, who reminds Scrooge of the opportunities for love and friendship he forfeited in his youth for the sake of money. One is the spirit of Christmas present, who gives Scrooge a glimpse at Mickey's family, which includes Tiny Tim, a lad who needs a crutch to walk. Finally comes the spirit of Christmas yet to be, and Scrooge finds himself in a graveyard where he sees Mickey, whose eyes are filled with tears for the loss of Tiny Tim. Then Scrooge sees a pair of weasels digging a fresh grave. "Never seen a funeral like this one," they say. "No mourners, no friends to bid him farewell." When Scrooge walks over to inspect the tombstone, he sees that it bears his own name.

In a state of panic, he awakens and finds himself in his own room. Then suddenly church bells announce that it is Christmas Day. With the perspective given him by the spirits, Scrooge is now a new personality. He is overcome with joy. He runs into the streets, showers money on the rat and the mole, who are still collecting for the poor. He encounters his nephew in a cart and declares how much he is looking forward to coming for dinner. And he purchases a bag full of gifts to take to the Crachit family. When he arrives, he feigns his old grouchiness. But before long, he declares that he is giving Mickey a raise and making him a partner in the business. The story ends with Tiny Tim and the other Crachit children sitting in Scrooge's lap—and all is as it should be on Christmas.

Just as Scrooge learns a lesson in perspective in this story, so do the eyes of Mickey Mouse suggest that quality in his character. Without abandoning his initial sense of wonder, without negating his acquired sense of focus, Mickey now has the wisdom of a sense of perspective that values life for its relationships and its larger dimensions of meaning.

And that is how God intends life to evolve for each of us. There comes a time when the experiences of our days teach us the lesson of perspective—turning the mirrors that can deceive us into thinking we are at the center of the universe into windows that open onto a larger landscape of truth.

When Jesus talked about the eye being the lamp of the body, it was in the context of responding to the light that comes from God. When we bring wonder, focus, and perspective to life in the light of God's kingdom—responding to that kingdom with integrity, singleness of purpose, and the totality of our being—our eyes have served us well. "If then your whole body is full of light, with no part of it in darkness, it will be as full of light as when a lamp gives you light with its rays." *(Luke 11:36)*

Four thousand runners began the Madrid marathon in 1985. At the end, there were two 36-year-old men leading the rest. They were very close friends. Suddenly, almost at the finish line, one of them began experiencing severe cramps and couldn't go on alone. Incredibly, his friend stopped, picked up his buddy, and carried him across the finish line.

The finish line of life is not the point of victory over our fellow human beings, but, rather, the bond between us that offers the perspective to see every shared experience of compassion as a victory.

An old story tells of a man who arrives in heaven and is shown into God's office. An enormous window looks out upon the earth. As he waits, the man studies the scene: At first, he's filled with wonder. It's a beautiful planet with blue waters, green forests, white clouds. Then he focuses more closely. He sees human beings despoiling the earth with selfishness and greed, exploitation and war. He closes his eyes and turns away. "If I were God," he mutters to himself, "I'd blast that globe out of the sky and start over."

Then a voice behind him says, "Put on my glasses." He

sees a pair of glasses on a desk, goes to put them on, then walks back to the window. This time he sees things he never saw before—a quiet act of kindness in the shadows, a courageous sacrifice for the sake of justice, a hidden potential in a human soul, a loving embrace in a humble place. And suddenly he feels a great compassion for this lost and lonely humanity. The voice behind him says quietly, "Until you see what I can see, you cannot feel what I can feel."

So it is that we receive the promise of our destiny when our wondering eyes begin to focus with the perspective of God's eyes—when we can look at life from the vantage point of faith and hope, forgiveness and love—and see that God shines upon every darkness in our lives with the emancipating light of his kingdom.

SOME QUESTIONS TO CONSIDER

1. What is something wonderful that happened to you last week?
2. Would you be willing to go on a plane ride with Mickey?
3. What are some of the worst things on which a person's life can be focused?
4. Should Mickey have told the king the truth, that it was flies rather than giants that he slew?
5. How has your own perspective changed during the past year/decade?
6. Have you ever known someone whose life changed as dramatically as Scrooge in *A Christmas Carol?*

CHAPTER 20:

THE TEMPER OF DONALD DUCK

Again he entered the synagogue, and a man was there who had a withered hand. They watched him to see whether he would cure him on the sabbath, so that they might accuse him. And he said to the man who had the withered hand, "Come forward." Then he said to them, "Is it lawful to do good or to do harm on the sabbath, to save life or to kill?" But they were silent. He looked around at them with anger; he was grieved at their hardness of heart and said to the man, "Stretch out your hand." He stretched it out, and his hand was restored. The Pharisees went out and immediately conspired with the Herodians against him, how to destroy him.

Mark 3:1-6

In 1934 Walt Disney Studios released a new film in its animated series called the Silly Symphonies. It was the story of *The Wise Little Hen*, and it introduced to the public an irascible duck named Donald. In stark contrast to the warm congeniality of the man who provided his voice for more than half a century—Clarence Nash—Donald's screen debut depicted him as a thoroughly shifty and shamelessly selfish rascal.

When a mother hen and her chicks plead with him to help

them plant their corn, Donald refuses with the words, "Who—me? Oh, no! I got a belly ache." Later when she returns to ask him to help them harvest the corn, Donald has the same excuse. Finally the hen prepares a great banquet—with delicious corn soup, corn muffins and corn bread, and fresh ears of corn slathered with butter. When she comes to invite Donald, he pretends to be sick again, until he hears her invitation to the feast. Then he makes a remarkable recovery. But when he arrives at the banquet, he receives what any duck with a belly ache might require: a huge dose of castor oil!

In a broad sense, the story of *The Wise Little Hen* is somewhat reminiscent of the story Jesus told about the wonderful banquet—which was his image of the kingdom of God—from which certain guests were excluded simply because they kept making up excuses for themselves. *(Luke 14:16-24)*

At any rate, this devious duck with his distinctive voice caught the public's fancy and made a second appearance that year in *Orphan's Benefit,* co-starring with a 6-year-old established Disney star named Mickey Mouse. It was Donald who stole the show as a fallible stage performer who loses both his composure and his temper when a juvenile audience of orphans starts to heckle his performance. From then on, Donald's career was assured, and he became one of the most popular cartoon characters in the world.

What fascinates us about Donald? Clearly, I think, Donald reminds us of a part of ourselves—that irritable, yet vulnerable, part of you and me that has to cope with obstacles, antagonists, and the unexpected in life.

And just as the gospel is intended for you and me, so it speaks to those qualities in us of which Donald reminds us. When we laugh at his predicaments, we're spontaneously sanctifying some very crucial lessons in life—moral lessons that Jesus himself would have us learn.

One of them is the ever-present danger of allowing our temper to get out of control. One of Donald's most prominent character traits has always been his explosive temper—punctuated by sputtering fits of inarticulate quacking. Donald's temperament has an exceedingly short fuse. It doesn't take much to set him off. And once Donald loses his temper, the consequences are usually disastrous. Whether it's a leaky faucet or a rainy day, a stalled car or a slippery sidewalk, two pesky chipmonks or three mischievous nephews—it only takes a few moments of frustration, and Donald is likely to blow his top.

In one of his movies, called *Cured Duck,* his girl friend Daisy even tells him she won't go out with him any more until he learns to control this volatile temper. So Donald sends away for a machine advertised as a temper control aid. This machine proves to be a rather diabolical invention. It pulls every trick in the book—insulting Donald, taunting him, punching him.....all the time daring him to lose his temper. Miraculously, Donald somehow survives the test, and finally—with a certificate of self-control—he returns to Daisy's house. "It's the new me," he says, and his apparent calm in dealing with an obstinate window seems to bear him out. "Wonderful," declares Daisy, "I'll go out with you." And she disappears upstairs to get ready. When she returns to the top of the stairs, she's wearing an outlandishly ornate hat. When Donald sees it, he can't help but double up in laughter. Daisy—who, for so long, has been complaining about Donald's temper—explodes in a rage, and with a broom chases Donald right off the screen.

Donald and Daisy aren't alone. All of us have a temper. Every one of us gets angry. Even Jesus got angry. The oldest of the New Testament gospels doesn't mince words: "He looked around at them with anger." *(Mark 3:5)*

Dr. Karl Menninger has suggested that anger is the first

emotion a human being experiences. In his words: "Such evidence as we have indicates that, however sweetly we may interpret the fact, the human child begins his life in anger." [19] Birth removes a child from protection and peace, and suddenly thrusts him into an incomprehensible world of uncomfortable sensations and experiences. So his little face is red and wrinkled, his small fists are tightly clenched, and the cry coming from his tiny body is a fit of rage—not altogether unlike a tantrum from Donald Duck.

Thus it continues for the rest of our lives. We get angry. Our involuntary nervous systems don't comprehend the Ten Commandments, the Beatitudes, the Golden Rule. Our promotion is won by someone else, our business goes bankrupt, our car breaks down, our neighbor is noisy, our taxes are raised, our child is criticized, our spouse is late, our elbow is bumped—large and small, natural and unnatural, admit it or not, some things are going to make us angry.

A man came home on Thursday night to supper. His wife served him baked beans. He took one look at his plate, picked it up and threw it against the wall, then shouted at the top of his lungs, "I hate baked beans!" His wife was shocked. "I can't figure you out," she said. "Monday night you liked baked beans, Tuesday night you liked baked beans, Wednesday night you liked baked beans—and now, all of a sudden, on Thursday night, you say you hate baked beans."

Life is full of baked beans.....things that irritate us, and cause us to get angry. Anger is a natural human emotion—and, like all emotions, morally neutral in itself. It's neither good nor bad to be angry. The moral question is what we do with our anger. Are we more than our emotions? Do we control our anger, or does our anger have control over us?

Learning to control our anger doesn't mean simply pretending it doesn't exist. That, too, can be dangerous. Doctors tell us that certain physical maladies—such as ulcers, high blood pressure, migraine, obesity, even asthma—are often related to sustained and suppressed emotions, such as anger, with which a person refuses to deal. Furthermore, psychologists know that emotions which are outwardly denied and inwardly suppressed can lead to mental illness as well.

Learning to control our anger doesn't mean denying it. It's essentially a problem of management. Many centuries ago Aristotle made this observation: "Anybody can become angry—that is easy; but to be angry with the right person, and to the right degree, and at the right time, and for the right purpose, and in the right way—that is not within everybody's power and is not easy." [20]

Anger might be compared to gasoline. It can burn or explode. But if we can learn to control it, direct it, make it fire evenly and effectively—like gasoline in the engine of an automobile—its energy can move us, like the car, forward.

We live in angry times. A lot of people are angry about a lot of different things. But the tragedy is that so much of that anger serves no constructive purpose. Quite the contrary, its effect is frequently destructive. It's like Donald Duck losing his temper when a door is stuck— kicking the door, and causing the whole wall to collapse.

One of my college professors, George Bach, has written several helpful books about the constructive uses of anger in relationships such as a marriage. Anger, temper, quarrelling—they're all involved in a home, as in every social institution. But they don't have to be destructive. They can serve a positive purpose as long as their energy is directed toward solving a problem, rather than sabotaging a person.

When Jesus became angry at the Pharisees for their rigidity with regard to the sabbath, he didn't lash out at them. Instead, he unleashed the energy of that anger in an act of healing. Mark reports: "He looked around at them with anger; he was grieved at their hardness of heart, and (he) said to the man, 'Stretch out your hand.' He stretched it out, and his hand was restored." *(Mark 3:5)*

And this leads into a second lesson—central to the gospel—that I think Donald Duck's experiences repeatedly demonstrate. And that is the ultimate futility of endless retaliation. The running theme in so many of Donald's films is the battle that develops between Donald and some antagonist—maybe a bee, a bear, a rooster, a buzzard, a gopher, some ants, chipmonks, nephews. Sometimes Donald is the instigator, sometimes he's not.....but once the battle begins, the recriminations invariably build up to something catastrophic.

For example, in his film, *The New Neighbor,* Pete—a Disney "heavy"—moves next door to Donald. Pete proves to be an undesirable neighbor indeed—dumping garbage on Donald's lawn, allowing his dog to damage Donald's fence, borrowing Donald's tools and leaving them out in the rain. Donald loses his temper and begins to retaliate. When leaves from Pete's tree fall on Donald's yard, he burns them and blows the smoke onto Pete's laundry. Furious now, Pete turns the hose on Donald—then Donald maneuvers the hose into Pete's trousers, causing them to expand and burst. The battle continues to build until it becomes a media event, with television cameras covering the acts of destruction as garbage cans fly and trees topple and both properties are eventually destroyed. The film ends with both neighbors forced to leave the neighborhood in disheveled defeat. Where they couldn't live together, they couldn't live at all.

A husband was reported to have struck his wife in the course of an argument. An acquaintance asked him about it later. "Did you really hit her?" "Yes, I did," said the fellow. "I got tired of her screaming at me, so I popped her a good one. It taught her a lesson, too. I didn't see her for five days. Then, on the sixth day, I could see her a little out of the corner of one eye."

In reality, of course, it's no laughing matter whenever violence erupts in human relationships and becomes a chain of retaliation. That is what's happening in so many troubled areas of the world today—ancient rivalries kept alive by new acts of recrimination, igniting further retaliation and more violence. And the potential repercussions of this vicious cycle in a nuclear age are catastrophic.

There's an ancient legend about an angel who came to visit two men. The angel promised to give them both a gift, whatever they wished for. In fact, he would even go so far as to give the second man a double portion of whatever the first man wished for. Both men began to imagine what they wanted.....but neither man would speak, because he wanted the double portion. Each tried to be courteous at first. "Please go ahead," they said to each other. Soon the tone became angrier—"You first!" One thing led to another, and before long, they were fighting each other. Finally one had the other by the throat, and threatened to choke him to death unless he made his wish. "All right," coughed out the other, "I'll make my wish. I wish to be struck blind in one eye!"

When our concern for vengeance overshadows every other concern, we're participating in our own destruction. One line I especially remember from the movie *Gandhi* was the Mahatma's observation that in a world that retaliates "an eye for an eye," everyone will eventually be blind.

This is the focus of Jesus's ethic: "You have heard that it was said, 'An eye for an eye and a tooth for a tooth'. But I say to you, Do not resist an evildoer." *(Matthew 5:38-39)* Learn the lessons of love.....the kind of love that embraces, not only those who love you, but even those who don't—even your enemies. Learn to love goodness even more than you hate evil. The vicious cycle of evil endlessly retaliating against evil can never be broken unless, somewhere, somebody refuses to go on with it.

This is the central message of Shakespeare's drama, *Romeo and Juliet.* It's a play about the antagonism between two powerful families long ago in the Italian city of Verona. The Capulets and the Montagues hate each other. Each family retaliates wrong for wrong, violence for violence, and the spirit of vengeance makes of them deadly enemies. But, as fate would have it, Romeo, the son of old Montague, falls in love with Capulet's daughter, Juliet. In the end, through a tragic twist of events, both children are dead. In the final scene—the climax of the drama—Capulet and Montague stand together. Learning the fate of their children, they are shamed by Romeo and Juliet's tender and beautiful romance. The tragic love succeeds in finally breaking the vicious cycle of retaliation. In that final moment of the drama, Capulet says, "O brother Montague, give me thy hand."

What Shakespeare teaches us with tragedy, Donald Duck teaches us with comedy—and Jesus declares to us about eternity: that the world's feuds can never end, and the vicious cycle of violence retaliating against violence can never stop until someone refuses to respond to hate with hate, and chooses instead to respond to hate with love.

But now, there's a <u>third</u> and final lesson I believe Donald represents. Indeed, I think it's his most redeeming quality. Donald—however short his temper, however prone to mutual exercises in demolition—is, nevertheless, a duck of rugged determination, because he's forever <u>driven by hope</u>.

His years have matured him, as the years should prod all of us closer to maturity. Donald today is no longer the self-absorbed juvenile who once refused to help the Wise Little Hen. He's learned the meaning of responsibility. He's served his country in educational and motivational films in wartime and peace. He's helped to promote international understanding through motion pictures such as *Saludos Amigos* and *The Three Caballeros.* He's appeared in films on behalf of volunteer charities, government bonds, accident prevention, fire survival, and more.

Many of Donald's best films depict a duck besieged by disaster in the line of duty. He may be a fire chief trying to cope with a fire that breaks out in his own station. He may be a forest ranger trying to save the trees from a beaver invasion. He may be a blacksmith trying to shoe a stubborn donkey. He may be a lighthouse keeper trying to keep the lantern lighted. He may be a clock cleaner, or a plumber, or a boat builder, or a scoutmaster, or a riveter, or a logger, or foster parent for a kangaroo. Whatever his duty, Donald can count on trouble. And we can count on Donald to persist—in the words of Shakespeare's *Hamlet*, to "suffer the slings and arrows of outrageous fortune"—because he's driven by hope. Even when everything goes wrong, Donald is still determined to make it right.

And that perspective goes directly to the heart of the gospel itself—the promise of a final victory that sanctifies life with determination and hope. Emily Dickenson wrote these words:

> "'Hope' is the thing with feathers -
> That perches in the soul -
> And sings the tune without the words -
> *And never stops - at all -*"[21]

Life is rife with surprises. Some of them bring tears. Some of them bring joy. Hope is the vision of a winning score.....seeing beyond the disappointment of the moment to the dream of tomorrow.....beyond the crisis of the present to the assurance of eternity.....beyond the Cross of Good Friday to the triumph of Easter morning. Hope is our claim on the truth that, no matter what happens, the future ultimately belongs to God and to the priorities of God's kingdom.

Therefore, hope becomes God's claim upon our lives.....as God seeks to engage us in the struggles for justice and peace, dignity and reconciliation, healing and compassion. God's work is our work—collectively through united efforts such as the Church—and individually through our own determination to serve the values that hope makes possible.

In 1964 a twenty-seven ton freighter, the Al Kuwait, sank in the harbor of Kuwait. It might have been abandoned except for the fact that it went down with a carload of 6000 sheep, whose carcasses represented a health hazard to the harbor area. In a short time they would poison the supply of drinking water. The only hope for avoiding a major potential health hazard was to bring that sunken ship back to the surface.

A Danish inventor by the name of Karl Kroeyer had a proven genius for solving problems. His inventions had earned him a respected reputation for trouble-shooting. So the ship owners turned to him for a solution. Was there any hope? Kroeyer studied the situation and assured them there was indeed hope.

Immediately Kroeyer dispatched a small vessel to Kuwait Harbor. It carried a long injector hose and 27 billion polystyrene balls, which were blown into the hull of the sunken ship. The bouyancy of the balls eventually counterbalanced the density of the vessel. Within twenty-four hours the ship had been raised. The impending disaster was averted. Indeed, subsequent ships all over the world have since been salvaged by the "Kroeyer" method.

Where did Karl Kroeyer get his brilliant idea? Donald Duck! After being presented with the problem, he happened to remember a Donald Duck comic book published in 1949. It contained a story in which Donald successfully salvaged a sunken yacht by filling it with ping-pong balls! That fictional challenge to Donald Duck inspired the Danish inventor to avert a serious disaster. It framed a gift of hope.

So today may we cling to that hope of a better world—where fewer lives may sink under the seas of poverty and warfare and ignorance and loneliness and despair. May we join the rescue teams of humanity.

And may we have the determination of the world's most famous and beloved duck—who, fallible though he may be, is forever driven by hope. For hope is the child of faith and the parent of love.

SOME QUESTIONS TO CONSIDER

1. Is there something that habitually causes you to lose your temper?
2. Do you suppose we would like Donald more if he never got angry?
3. What ongoing feud—exchange of retaliation—in the world today would you most like to see ended?
4. If you had been Donald when Pete acted as such an undesirable neighbor, what would you have done?
5. What is the thing you hope for, more than anything else?
6. Have you ever gotten a brilliant idea from a fictional source like a comic book?

REFERENCES

1. *The Disney Films* (3rd Edition), Leonard Maltin, Hyperion, p. 32.
2. *The Life and Legend of Jay Gould*, Maury Klein, The Johns Hopkins University Press, 1986, p. 96-97.
3. *Supreme Folly*,Rodney R. Jones and Gerald F. Uelmen, W. W. Norton & Company, 1990, p. 171.
4. *Frank Frisch*, Frank Frisch as told to J. Roy Stockton, Doubleday & Company, Inc., 1962, p. 274.
5. *The Miracle Worker*, William Gibson, Bantam Books, 1962, p. 118.
6. *Modern Maturity*, July/August 1996
7. *The Man to See*, Evan Thomas, Simon & Schuster, 1991, p. 390.
8. *WW II*, James Jones, Grosset & Dunlap, 1975, p. 205
9. *Thomas Jefferson- A Well-Tempered Mind,* Carl Binger, W. W. Norton & Company, 1970, p. 66-67.
10. *Give The Man Room*, Robert J. Casey and Mary Borglum, The Bobbs-Merrill Company, Inc., 1952, p. 85-86.
11. *Focus on Infinity* (A Life Of Phillips Brooks), Raymond W. Albright, The Macmillan Company, 1961, p. 349.
12. *The Open Door*, Helen Keller, Doubleday & Company, 1957, p. 31
13. *A Gentle Thunder*, Max Lucado, Word Publishing, 1995, p. 86-87
14. *Wind, Sand and Stars*, Antoine de Saint-Exupery, Time Life Books, 1965, p. 96 [copyright 1939, 1940, Harcourt, Brace & World, Inc.]
15. *Caesar and Christ*, Will Durant, Simon and Schuster, 1944, p. 642
16. *Encyclopedia of Walt Disney's Animated Characters*, John Grant, Hyperion, 1993, p.26.
17. *The Illusion of Life*, Frank Thomas and Ollie Johnston,

Hyperion, 1981, p. 447-448.

18. *Holy Humor*, Cal and Rose Samra, Thomas Nelson Publishers, 1997, p. 14.
19. *Love Against Hate*, Karl Menninger, M.D., Harcourt, Brace & World, Inc., New York, 1942, p. 9.
20. Quoted in *A Treasury of Sermon Illustrations*, ed. Charles L. Wallis, Abingdon Press, 1950, p. 16.
21. *The Complete Poems of Emily Dickinson*, ed. Thomas H. Johnson, Little, Brown and Company, 1960, p. 116.

ORDER FORM

Additional copies of ***The Gospel According To Disney*** may be ordered from your bookseller or directly from the publisher:

Longfellow Publishing
P.O. Box 312
La Canada, CA 91012-0312

When ordering from the publisher, please remit $15.00 for each copy ordered plus $3.00 shipping for the first book and $1.00 for each additional copy.

Please send me ________ copies of ***The Gospel According to Disney.***

Enclosed is $ ____________________
($15.00 for each book, plus $3.00 shipping for the first book and $1.00 for each additional copy)

____

Name ____________________________________

Address __________________________________

City ______________________ State _____ Zip ______

Telephone ______________________________________

___ (Check) Please inform me of future publications in this series.

For more information on Longfellow Publishing, please visit our WEB site: http://www.longfellowpublishing.com